BEWARE THE

Red Flag Man

Beware the Red Flag Man

What Mothers Wish Their Daughters Could Know

JANA COLE BERTRAND

BROWN BOOKS
PUBLISHING GROUP

Beware the Red Flag Man

What Mothers Wish Their Daughters Could Know

Manufactured in the United States of America

For information, please contact:

Brown Books Publishing Group
16200 North Dallas Parkway, Suite 170
Dallas, Texas 75248
www.brownbooks.com
972-381-0009

A New Era in Publishing™

ISBN-13: 978-1-934812-08-2
ISBN-10: 1-934812-08-0
LCCN: 2008921617

1 2 3 4 5 6 7 8 9 10

Dedication

This one's for the girls, my daughters:

Karri Lee

Kimberly Cole

Lauri Ellen

Sarah Elizabeth

Amy Hope

Lindsey Ruth

Emily Gail

*You will recognize your own path when
you come upon it because you will suddenly
have all the energy and imagination you will
ever need!*

Jerry Gillies

Table of Contents

Acknowledgments

I would like to thank my daughter Amy who kept asking and encouraging.

I would like to thank Milli Brown for letting me in the door and giving me a chance.

I would like to thank Dr. Janet Harris, the world's best editor without a doubt, for her unbelievable support and patience in allowing me to discover for myself.

Because of her:

"I may not have gone where I intended to go, but I think I have ended up where I intended to be."

Douglas Adams

Preface

All truths are easy to understand once they are discovered; the point is to discover them.

Galileo Galilei

eware the Red Flag Man relates to any woman in her quest for a meaningful, peaceful life, either married or single. Whether in personal relationships or in the workplace, you will inevitably encounter a Red Flag Man. This book will help you to make important discoveries for yourself as you learn how to identify him, realize how you are affected when you are with him, and know what you need to do for yourself to maintain your self-confidence and self-respect.

If you knew there was something you could do to prevent one type of horrific pain and sorrow from entering your life and the lives of your future children, would you do it? I have good news for you. You can. *Beware the Red Flag Man.* Though not as simple as it may sound, the process of learning about a Red Flag Man and using what you have learned can spare you needless, perilous ramifications. Because of the poor choices women make in men, divorce continues to destroy lives, especially those of innocent children.

A dear friend recently said, "I guess I will have to pay for my wrong choice in a man for the rest of my life." She sat alone, exhausted, and sad on Labor Day after working double shifts all weekend to pay her never-ending bills while her grown children enjoyed a weekend on the coast with their dad and his new wife on their sailboat. Her situation could have been prevented had she been more aware of the dangers of the Red Flag Man she married thirty years ago. This book is written to inform and educate you in identifying a Red Flag Man and spare you similar and unnecessary pain.

Beware the Red Flag Man gives a new term to a type of man that has been around since the beginning of time. I'm sure there were Red Flag cavemen, but, out of necessity and survival, women had fewer options. For modern women, marriage is more of an option than a necessity for survival. That fact allows you to choose more carefully, enjoy your life totally, and never need to settle for less than you deserve in a man.

Beware the Red Flag Man not only offers updated, appropriate terminology but also describes the criteria needed to identify such a man in your midst. Exploring his ten identifying characteristics will greatly help you in discovering the Red Flag Man for yourself. Pondering the effects of being with him will lead to serious self-examination and introspection. Discovering the impact he has on you emotionally, mentally, and physically will help you understand the magnitude of the potentially serious, personally damaging consequences resulting from being with a Red Flag Man.

Your mother, as a trusted and concerned bystander with a wealth of knowledge and experience, desires to spare you from making such a mistake in your life. You need another pair of eyes and a rational brain to see the truths evolving around you, and that person is possibly your own mother, a close relative, or a trusted friend. Yes, you are a modern woman, but the complicated and often subversive antics of a Red Flag Man have fooled many a world-class woman and led her into disastrous mistakes and even dangerous situations. Learning from women who have gone before you could be the critical key in sparing you such sorrows.

The final section of the book describes what you need to do for yourself in becoming an empowered woman. You will need to be smart, sure of yourself, strong, safe, and prepared for your future, alone or with the right man. Making wise choices will help you attain what most seek, a meaningful, peaceful life full of love, kindness, and acceptance. You will learn how to accept help from those who see more clearly and love you dearly, in order to avoid pain and horrendous sorrows caused from being with the wrong man.

Armed with knowledge and the new understanding of the Red Flag Man from discovering him for yourself, in addition to the wisdom gleaned from those who love you, you can confidently enjoy your own beautiful life while preserving your personal dignity, married or single.

What Mothers
Wish Their Daughters
Could Know

*We choose our joys and sorrows long before
we experience them.*

Kahill Gibran

What is a Red Flag Man? Why would mothers want their daughters to know about him? How can your choice in a man affect your joy or sorrow years down the road? Women from all walks of life and levels of education have asked such questions and for good reason. Discovering the answers for yourself through reading this book will prove invaluable in your quest for a happy and peaceful life—with or without a man.

Most already understand the concept of red flags signaling uncomfortable feelings in the pit of your stomach, intuitive warnings to keep you safe in relationships. *Beware the Red Flag Man* extends that to defining a particular type of man with ten distinctive characteristics that will alert you what to watch for. Such vital information is critical, not only for your safety but as a significant aid in one of the most important decisions you will ever make.

Mothers want their daughters to know of the early and often subtle signs of the harmful characteristics of a Red Flag Man, such as lying, cheating, controlling, as well as being verbally, emotionally, or physically abusive. They want them to be aware and cautious of unstable, unhealthy family situations and men who are too focused on themselves and material possessions. Mothers want their daughters to be adequately and skillfully able to meet the task at hand and to be smart, sure of themselves, strong, safe, and prepared to have a great future. Through no fault of their own, daughters are often clueless when they begin dating. Many are already at risk, coming from unstable or broken homes and lacking satisfactory examples.

When dating begins, their mothers' worries have just begun, and in a way, so have theirs. Attempting to navigate through the tumultuous dating years in search of a lifetime mate and partner proves complex. Mothers, as prime consultants, can offer priceless help for their daughters in making such a vital decision.

The expression "Red Flag Man" may be new, but further investigation of the term can prove priceless in a woman's search for "Mr. Right." Learning all about the Red Flag Man will give you knowledge necessary to make wiser choices. Most importantly, you will learn about standing up for yourself and what you deserve in a relationship: love and respect. You will learn about drawing lines to define important personal boundaries.

Several of my seven daughters recently got together

and reminisced about the literal lines they had in their rooms and closets growing up. They put masking tape down the middle of the room, closet, and shelves. Defining their space left no question about where each one's space began and ended. They already understood a vital life lesson about protecting and respecting your own space which proves far more difficult with a Red Flag Man. Many other essential skills will be needed as you meet this Red Flag Man and get to know all about him, including recognizing how you feel and how you are affected when you are with him.

Not one of my ten children had mastered all the necessary driving skills when their driver's licenses arrived in the mail and they hit the streets of a big city. They all completed driver's education classes, practiced driving, and passed the required tests, but I still had reason to worry. One got her gears mixed up and backed into another car when she wanted to go forward. Another totaled her car as she tried to navigate getting out of her high school parking lot. They thought they were ready, but in reality they lacked experience.

Similarly, women today, through no fault of their own, are just not prepared or sufficiently educated when they enter the on-ramp of relationships and run into the Red Flag Man. This road loops around and changes directions; it has road-blocks, potholes, unexpected detours, and many directionless drivers who are going too fast, too soon and are too focused on themselves. Women trying to meet someone in such a state of mass confusion encounter complicated, perplexing situations, and they frequently lack the knowledge and skills to maneuver through the obstacles. They often end up crashing.

Help waits patiently on the side of the road, though often ignored and bypassed. A wealth of experience, full of logical answers and plentiful warnings, in the form of your mother, close relative, or dear friend waits to help you. Their hard-earned experience waits like a sturdy lighthouse by the stormy sea and can spare you from getting lost, injured, bumped around, and bullied on that treacherous road of relationships. Knowing what to expect, how you will feel, how you are affected, and what to do is difficult on your own.

Lunching with a good friend recently spurred a discussion of this problem common to many mothers and daughters: an inability to get daughters to listen and learn from experience. My friend expressed great concern over the Red Flag Man her daughter had dated many years and was hoping to marry. She feared that expressing her concerns would offend her daughter and drive her further in the wrong direction. Mothers want their daughters to benefit from their years of experiences and mistakes and enjoy better, improved lives.

My mother used to say, "Learn from mistakes so every generation can be better by improving upon the other." The key word here is "learn." You can learn and gain necessary knowledge to assist you in this serious area of your life the easy way or the hard way. Learning from the experiences of others certainly makes navigating the extremely challenging road of relationships easier and more pleasant.

Realistically, daughters often resist their mother's well-intended advice. Straining to be independent, they make the mistake of losing out on the very wisdom that could help them make better choices in men. This mother summoned her courage and carefully guarded her words. Her daughter immediately turned defensive, had a ready-made excuse for every concern, and exclaimed, "We'll prove you wrong." The point is not about "proving" anything but about gaining and increasing your knowledge to make wiser choices and avoid needless suffering.

Help is available if daughters take advantage of it when making a very critical decision with long-range effects on their future. Many who love you stand willing to share their hard-earned expertise, experience, and mistakes to help you learn. You will need all the help you can get to discover the Red Flag Man for yourself and then make prudent choices in your life.

Mothers, I know the majority of you greatly desire to help your daughters and sons as well. You will need patience to help your daughters learn about the Red Flag Man and how to deal with him. You will feel exasperated and helpless at times, but never give up.

If daughters won't always listen to their mothers, perhaps they will pause and lend an ear to another "mother" through the venue of this book. Lovingly dedicated to my seven lovely, grown daughters, these words pour out to inform and educate you to be able to recognize the Red Flag Man when you meet him and then help others to do the same.

If women today would listen and then make wiser choices, perhaps a dent could be made in the skyrocketing divorce rate, and they could lead serene, meaningful, productive, and abuse-free lives, single or married to the right man. *Beware the Red Flag Man* will give you a good idea of the realities involving Red Flag Men. It warns, alerts, and even empowers you as your knowledge expands while building your confidence, strength, and courage to choose wisely.

As a first grade school teacher, I enjoyed taking my class on a great spring field trip to our district's Environmental Center. Summer training had prepared me for our upcoming hike in the woods. It seemed easy to navigate the woods with our experienced trainer, but I worried about doing it on my own and getting lost with my class. They were depending on me to lead them. I did my homework, studying my packet and guidebook.

We had a great learning experience because of that preparation. Being prepared is a choice. Choosing a man to spend the rest of your life with certainly deserves your utmost attention, effort, and preparation. *Beware the Red Flag Man* will help you do your homework for such a major life decision. Help in many forms surrounds you as a woman if you but look and listen.

Assistance rests here in your hands in the form of a book that can serve as your personal guidebook, helping you to know a Red Flag Man when you meet him by offering a detailed description of his many obvious and not-so-obvious characteristics. You may have noticed and been concerned about such behaviors in men, but now you will have specific terms to apply to the situations. This information will enlighten you about what to watch for. You will learn to spot a Red Flag Man. He can be any charming, handsome guy. You will need to step back and see what is inside this Red Flag Man before proceeding because confusion often surrounds him.

Good choices in a man require more than a little luck. Consider all the steps you go through before buying a pet: studying pedigree charts, contacting breeders, reading about special diets, checking obedience classes, and doing other research. How much more important is it to consider all the characteristics in a man and assessing how you feel when you are with him *before* trusting him with you heart and soul?

Your education in Red Flag Men will continue as you read and explore what it feels like when you are with one. Having suspected he has some of the characteristics, you can now witness and evaluate how you feel and are affected when you are with him. When feelings come into play, you need to be most vigilant and attentive. You will feel significantly affected in three distinct areas: emotional, mental, and physical.

The changes in you while with a Red Flag Man are subtle yet recognizable with the proper knowledge. Knowing how you feel and why you feel that way will support you in making wiser decisions. You may have already noticed such feelings in your relationships, but you were not aware of their escalating dangers or where they originated.

There comes a time when you must choose what to do: ignore everything, confront him with the problems, seek counseling together, or draw the line. Gaining knowledge of what you deserve in a relationship will help you stand up for yourself. Each case is distinctive, depending on how much you have tolerated and how dangerous your situation has become. Having determined individually who you are and what you stand for will aid you in getting where you want to go. You will learn how being a self-empowered woman can help you avoid a Red Flag Man, learn to live with a Red Flag Man, or recover from the aftermath of life with such a man.

Mothers wish their daughters could know a Red Flag Man when they meet one, acknowledge how he makes them feel and how they are affected when they are with him, and understand what they need to do while maintaining their personal boundaries and upholding their self-respect and human dignity. Mothers also want their daughters to know their choices will determine their happiness, not only now but for the rest of their lives, and affect future generations.

Knowledge can help you make wiser choices in men.

Watching out for Red Flag Men will protect you but only if you use the knowledge you have acquired and then ask, "Mother, what do you want me to know?" Using vital information about the Red Flag Man combined with the voice of experience can make a difference in your life.

Dear reader, you may have your own stories about a Red Flag Man. I would love to hear any and all for possible inclusion in my next book.

Send your stories to contact@redflagman.com.

PART ONE

How Will You Know Him When You Meet Him?

What we see depends mainly on what we look for.

John Lubbock

He Toys with Truth

*A liar will not be believed even when he
speaks the truth.*

Aesop

The proverbial taking a cookie from the cookie jar before dinner has taught many a lesson on telling the truth. Such significant lessons define you as a person of character who eventually can be trusted and counted on. Recalling and reminiscing about those simple, highly valuable lessons will serve you well now in knowing a Red Flag Man when you meet him.

A favorite high school friend married her high school sweetheart immediately after college. Their dating years were fun yet tumultuous. He appeared to be there in body but left a communication void. Always unsure about plans, she could never count on him. He resorted to telling her what she wanted to hear to pacify her, then did what he pleased anyway. He did not openly lie to her. This Red Flag Man just omitted the truth. When she confronted him about the inconsistencies, her word battles were one-sided because he ignored her. "Saying nothing some-times says the most," Emily Dickinson said.

Many dishonest actions crept into this young couple's courtship but were ignored or tolerated. They thought they loved each other but eventually discovered love wasn't enough. I vividly remember their wedding day and the day she called to tell me of their divorce. They were the first good friends I knew to split up, and their sad situation left me upset and frightened. I questioned her when I saw her: "Was he like that when you were dating him? Did you know those disturbing things before the wedding?" She remained silent.

Signs were present at the very beginning for another young high school girl unknowingly dating a Red Flag Man. Little things occasionally concerned her, but she excused his rude, inconsiderate behavior, telling herself, "No one is perfect." Her parents noticed other underlying problems and had concerns right away. Only when it was too late would she finally understand and know exactly why her parents shared great concerns yet were unable to voice them.

This Red Flag Man "in the making" always showed up late for casual dates or formal occasions. He had his own time frame which showed lack of concern and respect for her and her time. His comment when she called to see where he was consistently was: "I am on the way." He would arrive hours late with confusing explanations. What he said did not jive with what he did. Noting lies, big or small, constitutes a serious warning as you define and defend your own self-respect and know how much to take and where to draw the line.

Gradually she began to notice things he said not matching what her friends said. He habitually misrepresented facts, always in his favor. The continual discrepancies mounted, but he turned it all around so that she was the one who had a problem. She submissively dismissed the issue to avoid further confrontation, felt puzzled, doubted herself, yet remained very much unhealthily attached to him.

She lacked sufficient knowledge and strength to stand up to the lies and demand to be treated respectfully and honestly. Daughters under such a Red Flag Man's spell need their mothers, friends, counselors, or therapists. Listening to their advice might make the difference in joy and sorrow for the rest of their lives.

Honesty ranks on the top of the list as an important character quality, especially in relationships. Understanding the importance of honesty and truthfulness will help you notice the words and actions of a Red Flag Man more carefully.

Consequences follow our choices. Years ago I watched a popular television show called *Truth or Consequences*. This quiz show exhibited the idea of mixing the quiz element with wacky stunts. Participants would attempt to answer a trivia question before the buzzer. If they missed it, a zany, embarrassing consequence awaited their team. Indeed, consequences surface in real life for truth or the lack of it.

Discerning truth, facts, reality, and sincerity in actions,

character, or words proves a portentous task. Its importance reigns paramount in today's society that is riddled with mass acceptance and tolerance for broken promises and convenient lies. Just because you subscribe to a truthful agenda, taking promises seriously, does not mean the Red Flag Man feels or acts the same way. Understanding his agenda is a continual learning process.

Promises are supposedly binding declarations made from one person to another to ensure stable relationships. Lies loom in direct opposition to truth, bringing destruction to all that is stable, honest, and good. Catastrophe results if both people in the relationship fail to hold the same principles of honesty. Are you the only "honest" one in the relationship? If so, heed this warning sign and pause.

In his book, *People of the Lie*, Scott Peck notes the cumulative effect by stating, "Lies confuse, deceiving others as they also build layer upon layer of self-deception." Even the smallest lie can explode into the biggest disaster if you aren't alert to the tiniest indiscretion. Red Flag Men see themselves above reproach and faultless. Lies get twisted, turned, and mixed up. Lying gets only easier with time and turns into a negative lifelong habit, especially with Red Flag Men.

Even some first graders I taught, at the ripe young age of six, mastered telling lies. Puzzled by the fact that half of my new student calculators were missing, I asked questions around the room. Some students had seen a few of the calculators at a certain little boy's apartment along with a set of frogs, insects, and snakes that I had not yet missed. The six-year-old boy shrugged his shoulders as if not knowing how the stolen items had gotten there. When I spoke with his mother that afternoon, she denied knowing anything. Facing the fact that trust had been breached saddened me. "I am not upset that you lied to me, I'm upset that from now on I can't believe you," said Friedrich Nietzsche.

Resorting to checking this young boy's backpack daily often resulted in discovering handfuls of things he had grabbed from learning centers or off my shelves. He would look up at me and say, "I have no idea how that got in my bag." Just as I checked that backpack, women need to check out Red Flag Men for signs of honesty. Mentally going over important details and checking out his stories to see if the facts match is a relatively easy place to start your critical discovery.

Consequences follow our choices.

Are you prepared to realize such facts in your relationship? Lies, even seemingly small, meaningless ones, prove to be warnings of serious character flaws which cause gigantic problems in relationships. Not facing such facts leads to disastrous, immeasurable consequences. If you experience the slightest lack of trust with a Red Flag Man, for any reason, that is a warning for you to be aware and watchful.

A very intelligent, self-educated man often told stories that weren't true. After bragging about a bogus trip to Europe, he received an invitation to give a speech about the trip at a local club. He agreed to do it. He had the entire room fooled and enthralled as he described his visit entirely from what he had read. We can only surmise the lies his wife and children endured over the years. After a while, he himself could not distinguish fact from fantasy. Hopefully you can make a distinction for yourself and avoid Red Flag Men who toy with truth.

One shocked wife discovered the father of her three sons had also fathered the baby of a nurse at the hospital where he worked. Somehow she forgot that she had been a nurse at the same hospital and had broken up this man's first marriage where he had his first two children. Why did she suppose that this Red Flag Man would suddenly be faithful, true, and honest? His basic character did not change despite her hopes and dreams. Lies tend to pick up steam like a sled sliding down a steep, snowy hill.

A Red Flag Man often deceives and convinces himself of the things he says while fooling others. Experts at disguise, Red Flag Men lead seemingly respectable lives. Noticing discrepancies in facts can cause you to think *Did I get it wrong? or Did I hear that right?* If you have resorted to questioning yourself, then you need to question the source. Liars have an uncanny way of making you feel like something is wrong with you to the point of making fun of punctuality, organization, and sincere honesty itself. You might get caught up and manipulated into lying yourself. If that happens, recognize another warning sign.

A friend's husband was chronically late to work. His office would call religiously every morning, wondering where he was because clients were there waiting on him. His wife felt pressured to answer the phone and say, "Oh, he is on his way." He was the boss and wouldn't lose his job, but his inconsideration caused stress and trouble at home and at work.

One day, his wife said, "No more!" She refused to answer the phone and carry on the ridiculous scenario another day. His lies had negatively affected her, causing her finally to draw the line. Had she been more observant in their early dating years, this issue could have been addressed and possibly helped.

Lying becomes a habitual way of life for Red Flag Men. Trusting your life with someone who does not tell the truth could prove risky. One family dreaded holidays every year. Most of the family would be gathered while they waited for the last group to arrive. The brother and his family would always say they were on the way, but hours would pass, food would spoil, and tempers would flare. This lie went on for years. No matter what time was decided upon, he and his family would be hours late. That proved to be only the tip of the iceberg for the multitude of problems involved with them. The lies compound with miserable consequences for everyone.

Smart women learn from the mistakes of others. Mothers need daughters to listen carefully. Can you trust your flesh and blood more than a Red Flag Man who has manipulated you to the point of disrespect towards those who love you most? These forewarnings of lies spell double trouble for you and deserve your full attention.

Unfounded trust is blind and dangerous. One Valentine's Day an independent florist discovered the magnitude of honesty in business dealings. Known for artistic and unusual arrangements and his pristine reputation, he had gradually built his thriving business. However, he did not yet have a staff large enough to handle the biggest floral business day of the year. As it can with your life, one wrong decision can ruin it all.

Smart women learn from the mistakes of others.

Trusting someone with something important makes possible losing everything. He hired a delivery service and entrusted them with all his beautiful, expensive arrangements. He worked literally all night to get the orders ready and organized for delivery. The delivery service demanded cash payment up front to do the job. He paid them and felt confident that all would go as planned. Unfortunately, the delivery service was a fly-by-night scam and took off with his money and his flowers. Upset customers were calling all day wondering what happened to their orders. He lost so much money he had to close his small store.

Dishonesty deals out some tough lessons. This catastrophe could have been prevented. The owner should have checked out the delivery service more carefully, called references, paid by check only, and made sure the delivery company was legitimate and bonded. The same applies to you and the Red Flag Man. Do all your checking up front to spare yourself horrendous consequences.

"I knew it all along," you might say, realizing that little lies matter and indicate character and moral flaws. Knowing and noticing are not enough. Appropriate action in dealing with this Red Flag Man characteristic up front can spare you great trauma and tragedy in your life. Things seem so clear in hindsight, but you can turn your hindsight into foresight. If you don't see the situation clearly, perhaps a family member or friend who loves you does. Mothers can help their daughters. They have learned invaluable lessons and greatly desire to share them if only the daughters will listen. Learning from mistakes and from shared knowledge benefits everyone. "We lie loudest when we lie to ourselves," said author Eric Hoffer. Be honest with yourself when you notice lies and discrepancies from a Red Flag Man.

Exhibiting characteristics of lying, deceit, and dishonesty spells devastation to any relationship. Honesty is still the best policy. Personally you possess the inner strength needed to stand for truth and honesty to avoid the painful consequences. The choice belongs to you. This is *your* life. You now have the beginning of simple and valuable knowledge to help you carefully observe any Red Flag Man that crosses your path, and your ears should perk up if something sounds suspicious.

You can easily tell if he lies about something for any reason. If his stories don't mesh, if tales seem too good to be true, or if basic promises aren't kept, you need to check them out. Red flags are flying. Use your knowledge and the assistance of those with experience to help you discover the truth now before it is too late. This unfortunate characteristic weaves a nasty web in all aspects of life, but it is especially lethal in relationships. Take the time and effort to observe him carefully. Do you notice any fabrications? Do his stories have merit? Has he compromised your honesty and integrity in any way? Have you noticed any discrepancies in what he says and then does?

Observe him in daily life dealings as well. How does he handle the IRS, or does he give an honest day's work for an honest day's pay? Are you totally and honestly satisfied with how this Red Flag Man handles himself concerning truthfulness? Honesty remains the solid rock on which to base lasting, meaningful relationships.

chapter two

He Battles Family Boundary Issues

*Of all the peoples whom I have studied,
from city dwellers to cliff dwellers,
I always find that at least 50 percent would
prefer to have at least one jungle between
themselves and their mothers-in-law.*

Margaret Mead

A nice girl began dating a handsome guy who was several years her senior. They shared many common interests and enjoyed one another's company. An unusual family attachment caught her attention and caused concern. She wisely stepped back to analyze this Red Flag Man, not allowing the excitement of new love to cloud her vision. What she noticed was a simple yet complicated family issue and a warning sign.

This man always talked about his dad—what his dad had, thought, did, didn't do, believed, and felt. The man still lived at home and seemed unusually enmeshed with his parents to the point of having no real identity of his own. She felt at his age he should be living more autonomously, making his own decisions, and living his own life. She guessed right. Being aware of such subtle warning signs will pay off when searching for healthier, more stable relationships.

A young bride found herself continually arguing with her new husband about his mother and her unusual interference in their lives. She felt their privacy being violated and sought his support in beginning their own life together. One night he backed her into a corner and laid out the facts, saying, "My mom and I are a package deal, and you married both of us." Shocked barely begins to describe her reaction. When she hoped to go to sleep with her husband at night, he was in another room talking for hours on the phone to his mom. He never grew up or adjusted from being "mama's boy" to become an adult, much less a husband.

Some umbilical cords just never get cut, and that should be a warning to you in a dating situation. "Good-by, Son. I wish you were still home with me where you belong." Those words were uttered by an overly protective, overly involved mother to a grown man with his wife and children in the car. It was unhealthy enough that she felt that way and was unable to let go, but yelling it out to her son so inappropriately crossed the line.

The disturbing words were not only hurtful but also prophesied what life would be like with such interference. Not only did it put undue pressure on the son, but also gradually drove an impenetrable wedge between the husband and wife, making a loving union impossible. Red Flag Men often have dysfunctional family interactions that can be visible during the dating stages of your relationship if you just scrutinize the situation more carefully.

If Mom cannot let him go, then you need to pay attention and watch out. This warrants a red flag. A couple had dated during high school, and he had given her a charm he earned in sports. His girlfriend wore it on a chain and appreciated the gift. Unfortunately, he asked for it back. Feeling puzzled, she returned the charm. Later she learned his mother had wanted it back and now wore it proudly. This uncompromising, iron-willed, even selfish mother would never let go of her son or his things, sabotaging any hope of future meaningful relationships for him. Red Flag Men are negatively affected by such overbearing mothers and rarely change or improve over time.

When you are dating, going to meet his family is significant in more ways than one and definitely a time for due diligence on your part. Such a momentous occasion perhaps signifies the progression of the relationship to the next level for approval from supportive family members. An astute woman views the meeting as a sneak preview of what her life might be like with that certain person and carefully observes his family interactions. In reality, you marry a family, each member having his or her own quirks and idiosyncrasies. In some Red Flag Man cases, the package causes you to lose before you even begin.

Another consequence of ignoring serious family dynamics issues is that in-laws become out-laws. In devious ways, they manage to set you up to look foolish and smear your credibility. They manage by confusing details, withholding important information, and leaving you out of everything to make you look negligent, unhelpful, and unsupportive. A friend was excited about a future in-laws' party. Following the cues she had received, she showed up dressed very nicely but found everyone else in jeans. Her fiancé shrugged his shoulders, pretending oblivion.

In the movie *Legally Blonde*, Reese Witherspoon gets invited to a party and is told to dress in costume. She arrives and is the only one in costume, looking ridiculous and feeling uncomfortable. Red Flag Man family situations will make you look the same way if you aren't observant and careful.

In some Red Flag Man cases, the package causes you to lose before you even begin.

Mothers more easily discern such folly and find watching their daughters endure such treatment difficult. They have mother-in-law stories of their own to tell, and you need to hear them. Not only will you feel a new respect for your own mother, but you will also have a better idea of what to watch out for with a Red Flag Man's family. Familial relationships, while you are dating or engaged, deserve your concentrated investigation and contemplation.

Unfortunately at such times, you may be blinded by romantic infatuation and too caught up in the glory of the moment to be level-headed and watching out for danger signs. Knowledge of boundaries, invasive parents, functional families, enmeshed families, and the critical differences between parenting and partnering await your individual investigation.

Sometimes you aren't sure what a normal family situation entails. Noting attitudes like respect, dignity, appreciation, warmth, and empathy will remind you of how relations should be in healthy, functional family situations. Also look for open communication, freedom to communicate, kind words, attentiveness, caring, and equality. Education in this area proves critical when getting to know a Red Flag Man.

There is much you need to know about him. No one would willingly walk into the middle of a hornet's nest, but sometimes that happens in relationships if we are negligent in scoping out the family dynamics of this Red Flag Man. Such special issues are addressed in *What to Do When a Parent's Love Rules Your Life*, a book by Dr. Patricia Love. She discusses warning signs and identifying families at risk.

Dr. Love urges us to watch for clear separation of boundaries between adults and children. Do the people in the family appear to support, nurture, and show tolerance to one another? Do they have fun together and share significant interests? Do the parents show genuine love and affection for one another, work out problems together, and have an agreeable financial partnership? Are love and assurance found there?

Be on alert for another important aspect of family life. During this getting-to-know-him time, you might notice the absence of "please" and "thank you" and other signs of rudeness. Valuable lessons in manners serve you well in getting along in life, just as the lack of them signals the opposite. Growing up, our eyes popped out when someone openly burped or belched or grunted for more food as opposed to saying, "Please pass the peas." Manners or the lack of them say a lot about a man and his family.

Showing respect, gratitude, and appreciation in familial settings cannot be taken for granted. Manners matter. Whether family members treat each other kindly and considerately will intensely affect relationships. The Red Flag Man may be lacking in this area. You can readily detect such behavior, and then you can discuss and work on issues together. Exhibiting manners or the lack of them sometimes reflects deeper, more serious background, cultural, or other issues you need seriously to consider.

The movie *My Big Fat Greek Wedding* used humor, while yet it presented an accurate idea of how close family interactions affect relationships and create unusual problems. One woman I know was not so lucky when marrying into an unfamiliar cultural situation. The glamour gradually faded over time for my friend. His family rejected her to the point of refusing to share a dinner table with her. Later, her daughter was left out of receiving gifts and felt equally unloved. She would never be able to understand the blatant discrimination. The husband's neutrality or support of the parents only worsened the doomed-from-the-start situation.

Complications can arise with Red Flag Man family scenarios. One woman unsuspectingly married into a Pandora's Box of an in-law situation. Over the years, she learned the hard way that her husband's brother detested her father because he was a successful business man, and she felt shunned by this in-law. The wife unduly bore the brunt of this man's intense antagonism for years, complicating her marriage, dividing devotions, and making her life miserable. The unspoken feud set the stage for chronic trouble. Though not her fault, it became her incessant suffering.

In retrospect, comments about her father along with jokes about her family had surfaced during their dating years. Indeed, you marry more than the man. You also marry into whatever his family thinks of yours. Initial negativity will spiral over the years, separating you from your own family while ostracizing you from his, basically leaving you alone in limbo.

Your desire for knowledge in the area of Red Flag Men can help you. Asking, listening, and thinking will be beneficial skills. A bill in the Texas senate was passed, making marriage licenses free if premarital counseling classes are taken. Even the state realizes the need for education before marriage.

It makes good sense to discuss and communicate openly about many things *before* tying the knot. Identifying potential problems arising from extremely different family backgrounds helps the future of living and loving together. Troublesome issues might be something as simple as coming from loud households as opposed to quiet or varying values and moral issues. Everyone differs in particular likes and dislikes as well as tolerance levels and personal preferences. Checking these out carefully in a Red Flag Man will help you avoid future heartaches.

Problems in family dynamics present a significant strike against you before you even start your new life together. Couples today need total support from family, extended family, friends, religion, and work. Living with an intangible strain, caused by a parent or sibling in either family, tugging at either partner distracts, divides, and eventually destroys the relationship. Having such dysfunctional issues divides devotion and creates continual wear and tear on the new couple.

Your love will not be enough to pull him from the impenetrable bonds of emotional incest or unhealthy parental relationships. Even living too close in proximity to family can invade your private life, eventually rendering it nonexistent. One mother-in-law had a key and visited her son's home whenever she wished. When she wasn't there, she called her son incessantly. The couple never had any privacy or a moment to themselves. And yes, the Red Flag Man son repeatedly defended his mother.

"Too tight" means there won't be an inch available for you to squeeze into. Sometimes a close-knit family appeals to those who come from broken homes. Caution and deeper inspection reveal somber concerns. Do people in the family say, "I admit it. I made a mistake?" Do they accept responsibility for their own actions? Does criticism give way to the expectation of perfection? If unjustifiable sacrifice is demanded of you in relation to his family matters, you may feel debased and demoralized. A good man would not require that of you.

Family dynamics can be key indicators of your future life with a man.

Family dynamics can be key indicators of your future life with a man. The reasons for some family interactions may be ridiculous, but they will be adhered to stubbornly and determinedly by such families. The recurrent conflicts will paralyze your relationship and dictate your life together.

Invisible bonds hold tightly despite how lovely, devoted, and charming you present yourself. Take careful note of family interactions, especially at holiday times. See how they handle privacy, basic manners, and consideration for others. How is criticism handled? What about teasing? Make the most of your sneak preview of your potential life. The choices concerning the Red Flag Man are yours. Consider the entire package before accepting it and making all of them part of your life.

Unhealthy attachments observed while dating a Red Flag Man indicate warning signs. When you notice unusual family dynamics or unclear boundary issues, consider such situations very carefully. Do unhealthy ties seem to be causing problems which should be addressed before the fact and not after? Does his relationship with any family members detract or conflict with his rapport with you? What example did his parents provide for him? Sometimes what you see is what you get. Every sincere effort on your part will serve to add to your knowledge and aid in your making wise choices concerning this Red Flag Man.

Do you notice any unhealthy, inappropriate family attachments? Does he lack proper autonomy? Are boundaries respected among family members? Are you welcomed and appreciated in his family setting? Families are a big part of relationships and can add or detract significantly from their success. Do you see yourself able to fit into the whole picture? The Red Flag Man's family issues need to be recognized and thoroughly addressed before you become permanently involved with him.

chapter three

He Is Preoccupied with Possessions

*The real measure of a man's wealth
is how much he'd be worth if he lost all
his money.*

J. H. Jowett

A couple who married during medical school went on to internship and residency programs. Though they enjoyed nice salaries compared to med-school poverty levels, their lifestyle varied only slightly. They moved from the tiny-box student housing to a house. They kept their old cars, lived simply, were debt-free, and established their priorities of family and each other. Most people don't even know they are both doctors with substantial incomes. You will not wonder with a Red Flag Man. He has to show and tell what he possesses.

A young man eyed the red Porsche driven by one of the cheerleader's fathers. At that crucial moment, he determined he wanted to follow in that man's professional footsteps by making a huge amount of money and driving a fancy, expensive sports car. That desire for material possessions fueled and motivated his every thought and action.

As time passed, he gradually accumulated many expensive things although he never felt satisfied and always had his sights set higher on more and better possessions. If you recognize this trait in a man, it is a red flag.

He became obsessed and insatiable in his search for the best of the best in acquisitions, buying the latest car, wearing designer suits, and having the most prestigious address. This Red Flag Man's quest will never end or be fulfilled. "There must be more to life that having everything," said Maurice Sendak, children's book author. The Red Flag Man's view reflects serious poor-self-esteem issues as well as old-fashioned greed and pride. Such qualities fail to establish wholesome, meaningful relationships. Can you see where you might not be at the top of his priority list?

Love has no monetary value. Material possession cannot replace human kindness, sincere concern, genuine interest, or true comfort. You can achieve that fine balance of material possessions and a healthy relationship. It is worth discovering with someone who can handle and manage finances appropriately and effectively with you. Carefully scrutinize the Red Flag Man's priorities along with the extreme means he will go to achieve them. Spending money for show can be a dangerous addiction.

With this characteristic, the signs surface more visibly and blatantly. Though seemingly obvious, they still can be missed if you are not alert in observing this Red Flag Man. What are his priorities? Be cautious not to get carried away with the thrill of a fancy convertible, flying in his private jet, or traveling to the Greek Isles. Things require upkeep and attention, and they often lead to wanting more and better things, eventually overtaking what really matters in life. Your challenge requires knowledge and awareness of where this Red Flag Man channels his energies. Too many material possessions with the resultant focus on them spells trouble for you.

Recognizing the difference between wants and needs is critical for living within your means. Our fast-paced, materialism-oriented society encourages you thoughtlessly to spend beyond your income by maxing out all your credit cards with the belief that possessions bring happiness. Many Red Flag Men appear to agree.

A less subtle example involves an opportunistic, materialistic Red Flag Man. He had worked his way through college and was looking at big loans to get through dental school. He met an attractive, accomplished attorney a few years his senior. They married, and she supported them through four grueling years of school. When he graduated, he divorced her and married someone he met doing his clinical rotation.

Another similar case involved a college friend. This Red Flag Man attended the private college because of a sports scholarship. He hooked up with my friend, married her, and enjoyed having her father's help through law school and being set up in a productive law practice through her father's extensive business network. He indulged in affairs over the years until one finally ended the marriage and the law career as he had known it. Perhaps this materialistic lifestyle is a foreboding of other hidden character flaws.

From all outward appearances and for all practical purposes, this particular woman had everything, materially speaking: a nice home, a fancy car, vacations twice a year, a country club membership, and every possible perk. Though a busy mother, she had plenty of extra time and could buy anything she wanted or needed at the nearby mall. No matter how much she bought, the empty, sad, and lonely feelings never subsided. Meaningless things failed as a substitute for human communication and kindness.

She would have given anything to have felt love and appreciation from her Red Flag Man husband. His busy agenda consisted of acquiring gadgets, cars, sound systems, clothes, computers, and workout equipment in addition to rising in corporate America but did not include time for his wife and family. He bestowed elaborate gifts as an outward sign of how well off, important, and generous he deemed himself to be.

"I think that humanity brings much misery on itself by the false value they put on things," said Benjamin Franklin. Somewhere along the way, Red Flag Men put false value on things over people, and that is exactly when problems occur. The loss of the human element is hurtful, but the overspending leads to an outlandish life style, financial issues, fundamental relationship disagreements, and a man sneaking around behind your back with his spending addiction.

A materialistic Red Flag Man maintains a desire for wealth and avariciousness with little interest in ethical or spiritual matters, and he is consumed with thinking about all those things. Some Red Flag Men cleverly and deceitfully go after women who have the financial resources that they desire and need. If they haven't made the money yet or have proven unable to get it, they go after women who have. Be warned. Preoccupation with money and things combined with dishonesty and beguiling charm spell big trouble with a Red Flag Man.

"It is preoccupation with possessions, more than anything else that prevents us from living freely and nobly," noted Henry David Thoreau. Such behavior also prevents you from having the stable, loving relationship you deserve. One Red Flag Man, planning ahead for his financial future, even managed to swindle an unsuspecting woman from behind prison bars.

At the insistence of a friend, a single woman started writing to a man in prison. A long-distance relationship ensued. She ended up visiting him regularly and sending him money weekly for years. As time for his release neared, they planned to marry and live in her home. She played a huge part in helping him readjust to society after his sixteen years in prison. She paid for everything as he got back on his feet. He later left this woman and their daughter after seven years. He had gotten all he needed from her.

The spending is often on your dime. This Red Flag Man has no problem spending your hard-earned money with or without your approval. Money issues put tremendous strain on relationships and are a big factor in divorces. The ensuing never-ending struggles create great tension and ongoing disagreements. Especially notable are expensive collections, addictions, hobbies, and gambling of any kind. You not only take the chance of being a golf widow, but you also may end up paying for the golf clubs and green fees. Red Flag Men often harbor voracious desires for spending, impressing, and endlessly acquiring things to gratify their own desires and schemes.

Where do you fit in his priorities?

You could owe even if you didn't spend. Red Flag Men easily seduce women into financial ruin. One woman was left near bankruptcy with almost a million-dollar debt. Luckily she sold most of what he had purchased on her credit over several years. She succumbed to allowing him to take out loans, build a new home, buy an expensive car, and live lavishly.

She finally woke up when he showed her the elaborate pool plans. Having great concern for their indebtedness and finally expressing herself, she put the brakes on once and for all. She finally drew the line and held to it, although three years had passed before she figured out what this Red Flag Man was doing. Then she discovered that financial issues were not this Red Flag Man's only vice.

This Red Flag Man, who seems like a prize, may turn out to be an empty package. Ultimately, the responsibility lies in your court to distinguish the priorities of a Red Flag Man bearing material gifts as he tries to catch your interest and falsely impress you. Can you step back from the glitz and glamour long enough to recognize him?

"The best things in life aren't things," observed Art Buchwald. Only basic things are necessary for living. A Red Flag Man's obsession with material possessions at all costs leaves little time for relationships and often continues dangerously throughout life. It can be a serious warning sign. Daughters, you would be wise to listen to mothers on this one.

Materialism has infused our entire society with unrealistic hopes and dreams that only lead to debt and extreme emptiness. Watching out for a Red Flag Man's financial priority list in the early dating process can reveal such issues. If things are more important than people, red signals are flashing. Consider carefully all the possessions flashing before you and then look further beneath the surface of this Red Flag Man. Seriously consider if he is after you for his own personal gain socially or financially. Where do you fit on his priority list? Are you both headed in the same direction, with the same financial goals and plans to reach them? Carefully thought-out answers now will save immense heartache and pain later.

One innocent girl grew up in a small town, never having the material things other children in her school had. This made her particularly vulnerable to a Red Flag Man who gave her expensive, desirable gifts. She succumbed to the overwhelming, beguiling temptation to indulge in them. Over the years, the resultant emptiness led her to serious addiction problems, finding no comfort in what had originally lured her.

Watch out for these warning signs in a Red Flag Man. Does he flash material possessions in your face? How does he pay for them? Do things seem to be his top priority? Is he overly interested in your bank account or credit limits? Is he preoccupied or obsessed with all those material possessions? Does he have expensive habits, hobbies, or collections? Does talking about his belongings dominate his conversation and thoughts? What are his true priorities in life, and where do you fit? Defining that now will spare you serious disappointment and unnecessary surprises later.

chapter four

He Takes Total Control

Time is the coin of your life. It is the only coin you have, and only you can determine how it will be spent. Be careful lest you let other people spend it for you.

Carl Sandburg

Marrying too young to escape an uncomfortable home situation, an innocent girl set up housekeeping and found security in her somewhat older husband who so capably took care of everything. He set the routines, house rules, kitchen guidelines, and budget, leaving her no input whatsoever. Owning only one car, he took care of the driving, going to work, doing all necessary errands, and grocery shopping.

She cheerfully turned all her efforts to baking and sewing exceptionally well. As children were born, he gradually and guardedly allowed her out of the house for the children. He added unusually severe restrictions to their children as they started school, regarding dress, make-up, and television. This Red Flag Man thought he was totally in control of his entire family. Battling the oppression, his children rebelled violently as teenagers, and finally, when they were grown and their mother could bear no more, she broke free of her Red Flag Man.

Another woman, a new mother of a son, recently informed me that she had separated from her husband because he exerted undue control and treated her disrespectfully. She now wants a better example and life for her son. She showed great courage and wisdom in demanding separation and counseling until things change. When they first met, his control and confidence swept her off her feet. Unfortunately after their marriage, that control turned overbearing, suffocating, and abusive. The red flags she missed initially had become intolerable to live with later.

Friends may scorn her for not trying harder, but both people need to try harder to make things work. He harasses her for depriving their son of an intact family and continues to manipulate, blaming her for everything as he still attempts to control her from afar. But she stands firm for her son and herself.

We might question her choice in men and whether she ignored the red flags. No one knows that except her. However subtly, the man exhibits totally unacceptable actions, inappropriate behavior, and a hypocritical persona. He portrays the typical Red Flag Man: suave, self-assured, knowing just what words to say. Underneath, he speaks only out of self-concern and has an agenda of control that is all his own. Everything is all about him. Likely it will never be about anyone else with a Red Flag Man.

You always return to one word: choices. Your knowledge can improve your choices and your chances.

Women today in manipulative, totally controlled relationships make sacrifices, endure tragic experiences, and pretend their lives are fine. Women who are silently being totally controlled in relationships may need outside help. When love loses its joy, we have to rescue ourselves.

The main tool for asserting control over another human being is the manipulation of words. Manipulative people are described as "sneaky," "needy," "underhanded," and "emotionally demanding." They tend to turn situations to their advantage and serve their own purposes. This Red Flag Man has been described as a wolf in sheep's clothing. Totally controlling everything leads to his twisting and turning facts against you, making you think you are crazy.

Ask your mother, "What do you want me to know?"

Red Flag Men use emotional tricks to control their partners. Feeling controlled does not mean something is wrong with you. Tolerating control and dominance over you and then blaming yourself for the troubled relationship is skewed thinking. Victims feel trapped and confused. To the outside world, your relationship appears perfect, but in reality such dominating treatment is oppressive and cruel, leaving you feeling miserable.

Master-manipulating Red Flag Men covertly cover

their tracks by appearing "normal." They say, "You can't get along with anyone. You don't know what you are talking about." The words "I love you" are meaningless without appropriate, consistent actions in daily life. Do you feel dominated and controlled to the point of losing basic freedoms? A woman called in to Dr. Laura recently and explained that her husband had not allowed her to buy one item of clothing or cut her hair for over four years since their wedding. Your mother might notice subtle tyranny before you do. She may have suffered its effects herself and strongly wants you not to have to do the same. Can you see how she would want better circumstances for you as her beloved daughter? Listen to her. Go to her and ask, "Mother, what do you want me to know?"

Red Flag Men literally charm you off your feet. Temporary blindness to reality makes it difficult to see the actuality of the extent of control in the relationship. Charm fascinates, allures, delights, and appears to be a very compelling attraction before evolving gradually into serious control and dominance. This domination takes over controlling a relationship with a stern upper hand. Historically, women slip into denial and inevitably attempt to cover up what is happening to them. In this situation, denial, if not overcome, can lead to disaster if warnings are ignored. Intellect, social savvy, and professionalism don't always signify emotional intelligence. You need more knowledge to render you capable of overcoming such denial so you can recognize the emotionally sound love you deserve.

As a woman, your inner spirit will speak to you. Learning to hear and trust it takes time and patience. Occasionally, an overly controlled woman gets a definite gut feeling that things have degenerated to uncomfortable, unacceptable levels with symptoms like being out of balance, stressed, and exhausted. Realize the situation when symptoms erupt and know you have options. Recognize the red flags. Listen to your own concerns.

Dangerous men can look exactly like regular men. These Red Flag Men are dangerous because they will stop at nothing to exert total control over you. Once a Red Flag Man infiltrates your life, unhealthy behaviors multiply like rabbits and then take over, making escape difficult.

Charm fascinates, allures, and delights before evolving into control and dominance.

Have you given up even one freedom to be with this Red Flag Man? Do you feel dominated or controlled in any way? Have you been isolated and kept from the family who raised you and loves you? Are you pretending things are great in hopes that they will improve someday? Do you feel trapped or confused and are not sure what to do about it? Are you silently terrified? Do you feel in any way uncomfortable about anything that this Red Flag Man has done or said to you? Have any lines been inappropriately crossed?

You are the master of your ship and the master of your soul. With knowledge, you can learn to take control of your own life and guard the freedoms that are innately yours. A peaceful life without manipulation or control awaits all who seek it. "I believe that we are solely responsible for our choices, and we have to accept the consequences of every deed, word, and thought throughout our lifetime," states Elisabeth Kübler-Ross.

Strength, courage, wisdom, and knowledge will combine to protect you from such control and give you the ability to recognize when it overtakes you. Do you notice that you are never consulted on any decisions no matter how insignificant? Is your opinion made to look useless or invalid? Have you lost having a say in your daily routine of life? Has the control stepped up to dominance? Does your gut tell you something is wrong? Do you feel ambivalent with how you are treated? Being in a healthy relationship will allow you the freedom necessary to be yourself. Never give that up for anyone, especially a Red Flag Man who will take total control in a heartbeat if you allow it.

He Uses Words as Weapons

*Yelling at living things does tend to
kill the spirit in them. Sticks and stones
may break our bones, but words will break
our heart.*

Robert Fulghum

A college girl was home for the summer and ventured downtown to take a new yoga class. Driving home in the dark, she found herself hopelessly lost in an unfamiliar part of town. Feeling somewhat panicked, she called a Red Flag Man. He was insensitive to her plight, made her feel stupid for being lost, and laughed, making a joke of her fear. She was desperately crying and became so hysterical to the point that he had to go find and lead her back to her apartment. If you experience any such bad behavior by a Red Flag Man, consider yourself warned.

A sweet, innocent, blue-eyed, red-headed little girl kept an important secret from her mother for years. In her elementary-school classroom, the blackboard looked blurry, and she could not see well. Luckily she was very smart, so she got by making the most of her listening skills and accommodating the best that she could. An observant, caring teacher finally noticed and talked to her about it. Devastated, she begged the teacher not to tell her parents. This child was terrified of having to wear big, ugly glasses and be called "four eyes." Luckily she got contacts and never had to hear those dreaded words.

Verbal abuse is another warning sign.

On the very first day of school each year, I announce one of the biggest rules in my first grade class by saying, "Absolutely no name calling." One cold, winter morning my students' behavior made me feel very proud of them. A cute, popular little boy walked in late with a multitude of tiny braids sticking out all over his head. He honestly looked like a character from the old comedy show *Spanky and the Gang*. I could hardly keep a straight face since he looked so funny to me. I wanted to call his mother and ask, "Why on earth did you do this to your child?" My well-trained students stared with bugged eyes but said not a word. They showed the respect they had been taught without even giggling. You deserve that same respect in every relationship.

Inappropriate name-calling hurts. With the passing of time and age, this obvious name-calling evolves into something more indirect, subtle, and even more hurtful to mind and spirit. Name-calling doesn't have to be a bad name or a curse word. You could be called "stupid" or "a klutz." One of my former students came from a great family where most of the children were honor students. He was above average but did not measure up to the competition at home.

His self-esteem was obliterated by playful comments from his Red Flag Man father. The siblings picked up on the example set and relentlessly taunted him. That translates to just another unfortunate by-product of this characteristic. It leads to being easily mimicked in negative, hurtful ways. Have you been made fun of in even the slightest way by a Red Flag Man? If so, red flags are waving in your face. Letting him know how you feel about it may cause him to think more carefully before speaking, but he will never know unless you bring it up for discussion.

A young wife had her hands full raising several children and managing their busy, active household. Her Red Flag Man husband rarely shared his thoughts or plans with her, causing undue stress and confusion as she planned meals and activities for the family. Whenever she finally coerced him into discussions, he almost always stubbornly took the opposite view from hers, no matter what the topic. The words he finally spoke to her were not what she needed to hear. Using words as weapons against her, he was always right and superior, and she was always wrong and inferior. This made her feel sad, downtrodden, and hurt while he appeared unscathed and the innocent victim.

These days almost everyone is familiar with verbal

abuse in one form or another, and unfortunately, they most likely have experienced it firsthand. Such abuse does not leave visible bruises or scars, and yet the subsequent suffering unfolds often in silence and is endured internally and privately. Verbal abuse comes forth as any undeserved statement of disapproval which can cause lasting scars. Physical wounds heal, but emotional wounds from verbal abuse can last forever unless treated with loving-kindness and, possibly, therapy. Verbal abuse is another warning sign.

Try to visualize the painful setting this kind of treatment creates. Discounting makes you feel worthless, ignorant, and wrong about everything. Trivializing makes your accomplishments seem insignificant. Consistently forgetting promises, agreements, and occasions involving you belittles your worth. Ordering denies any chance of equality in the relationship. Verbal abuse in all forms is insidious, unpredictable, manipulative, controlling, and damaging. Knowledge in this area can prevent a plethora of pain and help you determine where and when to draw that line to preserve your dignity and basic rights.

A beautiful young girl floated down a spiral staircase in her elegant prom dress. She was somewhat upset as her date arrived late as usual, and they had to hurry off to a pre-prom party. He neglected to comment about how she looked or the magnitude of the evening. She would suffer verbal abuse in many forms that evening and throughout the relationship with that Red Flag Man.

At the pre-party, the handsome couple strolled down

a walkway to a garden area bordered with votive candles and exquisite flowers. As they meandered over to the buffet table, he said something common to many teenage boys, "I hate this tux. I'd really rather be home watching my new TV." Nonetheless, the comment was rude and hurtful. Her plastered smile hid her feelings as he continued to evoke feelings of disappointment, confusion, and inadequacy. He repeatedly said, "I love you." But the words didn't mesh with his actions.

She had no name for what happened to her and felt as though something must be wrong with her. Instead of trying to communicate her hurt feelings to him, she overlooked it, tolerated it, and stuck around for more. She did not realize the impact of demoralizing, disrespectful treatment, which eventually made her feel crazy, inept, and worthless. She could not feel anything, much less special, as long as his verbal abuse continued to be directed at her. Unfortunately, she was oblivious to the spell cast upon her and the real intent of his verbal abuse: to maintain power over her.

Verbal abuse inflicts damage on its innocent victims. A very competitive Red Flag Man basketball coach drove his players to the limits in a negative way. During a game, if a simple mistake occurred, the player knew he would come out of the game and immediately face the rage of the coach. That coach was out of control, and he took his rage out abusively on the players on his team. They had to take it without a word if they wanted a chance to play, unless parents understood the coach's problem and stepped in to make changes. That is a warning sign.

We often think what we hear and act accordingly, for good or ill. Words can be powerful and make indelible impressions on our minds at all ages and stages of our lives. Recently our school had Field Day which culminates with a tug-of-war. I had pumped up my students, saying, "1 A is the best." I carefully lined them up with the strongest students first in the line, and they chanted, "1 A, 1 A, 1 A." They pulled down two classes who had male teachers tugging with them. Those pumped-up kids won the entire event and were ecstatic. The power of words can be great.

You will feel constantly under attack and on alert.

Verbal abuse in your relationship may be hard to define, but if you are diligent, you can notice how it negatively affects your life. Subtle changes will make you feel inferior, incompetent, worthless, and dependent. You will hear him say, "Do what you do best: just go to the grocery store. Nobody asked your opinion." The resulting skeleton of a relationship will be dysfunctional.

You will be accused of making a big deal out of nothing, not having a sense of humor, and being too sensitive. They go for the jugular by saying, "You're never satisfied.

You can't keep anything straight." Wrestling with the continual criticism will wear you down. You will feel constantly under attack and on alert.

Consider carefully the words of Stephen Fox, author of *The Double Message of Verbal Abuse:* "Love does not create verbal abuse. Dominance does." Beware of the control and dominance inflicted upon you with the words of a Red Flag Man who makes you feel confused and crazy. One danger of associating with Red Flag Men is that sooner or later you end up constantly on your guard, afraid that everyone will treat you like that. Such treatment has been described as "heart and soul mutilation." Real, meaningful, healthy love is nonexistent in this scenario.

Recovery from this type of treatment is possible once you realize what is going on. This knowledge you are building will assist you. We recently had very severe weather that included a tornado warning. The sirens were sounding, and people were told to take cover. Luckily the storm swiftly passed. The following day the sun came out as if nothing ever happened while the night before had brought hailstones the size of golf balls and high winds knocking down trees and tearing off roofs.

If we use the knowledge we acquire, we can possibly avoid the storm altogether and carry on or take the necessary steps to cope, negotiate, compromise, and work out the problems. Those suffering with verbal abuse in any of its many forms have options. Discussing your concerns with your mother would be a good one to try. "Destiny is not a matter of chance, it is a matter of choice," said William Jennings Bryan. You can choose to ignore serious Red Flag Man issues or face them head on.

Remember no one is perfect. We all make mistakes. Are yours tolerated lovingly or made fun of? Are you made to feel stupid or inferior in any way? Are obvious words withheld from you in a hurtful manner? Are you called hurtful names in private but treated differently in public? Do you feel dependent, worthless, or inept? Are you the brunt of unacceptable, degrading jokes or comments?

Do inappropriate words from a Red Flag Man to you cross the line, making you feel demoralized, oppressed, or worthless? Listen carefully to what is spoken and unspoken with a Red Flag Man. You choose what words you will hear for the rest of your life. Beware also of the tone Red Flag Men use to address you. Words and the way they are spoken to you matter. Beware of the Red Flag Man and the way he uses words as weapons.

He Inflicts Physical Abuse

The greater the power, the more dangerous the abuse.

Edmond Burke

A young woman married her prince charming and enjoyed a magical wedding. She glowed in a magnificent designer gown of Belgian lace, encrusted with pearls, and wore a veil connected to a tiny, delicate crown. Following the reception was a lavish buffet and dancing to a popular band, the couple left the golf course of the prestigious country club in a private helicopter. They were whisked off to catch a jet to a private island. The happy couple moved far away where "daddy" could no longer protect her. The Red Flag Man groom had a hidden agenda, involving taking over her vast bank account, trust fund, and inheritance, and then physically threatening and mistreating her.

Somewhere along the way in their courtship and dating days, she and her family missed some very important warning signs. Unfortunately, she found herself cornered, an innocent victim of cruel berating, terrifying accusations, and malicious threats. This Red Flag Man's physical abuse of this unsuspecting woman took her and her family completely by surprise, leaving her stunned and at a complete loss of what to do.

No parents could bear to have someone who claims to love their daughter harm her in any way. If your mother does suspect such abuse and then tries to warn you, ignoring her could be digging your own grave. Daughters, you are bright, educated, and living in a new generation. However, some things, like Red Flag Men, don't change.

If you are fortunate enough to still have your mother, you owe her the respect of listening to her when she attempts to warn you. Yes, she may be emotional or frantic if she thinks for a moment physical abuse has affected her precious daughter. Be grateful she cares enough to risk your turning against her, siding with the man, and never speaking to her again. Think long and hard before dismissing advice from your mother or someone who cares about and loves you.

Mothers watch out for their children even though they are grown. Hopefully, you've not had reason to worry about your grown children being physically abused by their dates or husbands. Unfortunately, such abuse tends to be hidden, and the abused person feels shame, blames themselves, and rarely reports the abuser. Early warning signs of danger you need to be attuned to would be sharp tempers, anger- or stress-management issues, and controlling attitudes.

A friend recently told me she had a volatile, verbally abusive relationship with a man who professed to love her. During one conversation, she confessed her back and neck hurt because the initial abuse had suddenly escalated, and her fiancé had pushed her down during an argument. Unable to contain his anger, he knocked her down and crossed the line. If a hand is raised to you, whether he hits you or not, that is a huge red flag.

What happened did not surprise her, considering he had previously grabbed her forcefully and raised his hand over her in a rage. Ignoring those warnings will continue to put her in harm's way. If she does nothing, this Red Flag Man will assume her apathy gives him unspoken permission, allowing the abuse to continue and leaving her life at possible risk.

A week later, she seemed unconcerned about the incident. She said he had apologized and, when his temper had cooled down, told her he loved her. This is the typical pattern for abusers. But she had no place to go, limited funds, and months of school left. She felt that staying was her only option until she could graduate and hopefully make it on her own. A Red Flag Man will not only physically abuse you, but he will also make you feel you have no place to go and no chance of living successfully on your own. You can sense when things are close to being out of control and you may be in danger.

Society seems to tiptoe around the nasty issue of physical abuse and all that it entails. Granted, the subject is offensive and appalling. The use of physical force against another person, whether injuring or risking injury constitutes physical abuse and can range from mere physical restraint to murder. Specific actions to watch for in a Red Flag Man are pushing, throwing, tripping, slapping, hitting, punching, kicking, holding, restraining, confining, assaulting with a weapon, burning, freezing, or throwing things.

If you are fearful, red flags exist.

Fear caused from experiencing such actions or being threatened appears in direct opposition to professed love. Physical abuse surfaces through fear, intimidation, and threats leading to physical injury. Physical assault or physical battering is criminal. You are not to blame for how the abuser acts or feels. You are, however, in charge of protecting yourself. If you are fearful, red flags exist.

Because many of us have nurturing natures as women, we may sometimes set ourselves up for abusive situations. Our minds guide us when we listen. Life is like a crazy maze at times, causing the line between "helping" and "being abused" to be thin and unclear. Abusive patterns multiply, becoming impossible to hide or ignore. Inevitably, the situation will demand to be dealt with and faced honestly. The aftermath, the fallout, the rubbish, and the sorrow will be left in your lap, and the scars could be on your face as well as your heart.

How much do you tolerate or put up with? At what point do you draw the line? Smart parents teach their children to make decisions before the fact and to know where that line not to cross exists. Practicing answers and actions for various dangerous and tempting scenarios can help anyone prepare for future incidences. Not every possible scenario can be imagined, but teaching basic principles of life to help them cope and make wise choices pays off in the end. Accumulating facts about the Red Flag Man will increase your knowledge and help you be better prepared to recognize that line and make wise choices of your own as well as protect your children and their future relationships.

Recognize the issue of your own personal space.

Recognizing the issue of your own personal space is vital. First graders know to respect each other's personal space and never to bother another person at school. Ultimately the lesson to be learned is one of respect, privacy, and moral character. As you discover the Red Flag Man for yourself, you will be prepared to know him when you meet him. You will know physical abuse cannot be tolerated. You may need to seek help to gather the strength to extricate yourself from such danger.

Sometimes our minds tell us to give up, but our hearts won't let us. Have you ever felt that way? Your mind and soul will help you determine the best and safest path for you. Being smart and watching out for warning signs will help keep you safe. Some women are desperate. Any man will do. They may be trying to escape an unhappy home life or are dealing with previous abuses in their lives. Others are concerned about their biological clock ticking away, giving them a sense of urgency that often clouds their vision and leads to mistakes in choices. The heart and mind battle while your life could be in danger.

Countless relationships border on abusive issues that over time have been disregarded or just accepted. Women of all ages suffer abuse from Red Flag Men who supposedly love them, and these women often accept worthless apologies. Gaining knowledge is necessary to help you know the Red Flag Man when you meet him, as well as where and when to draw that line. "It is not denial. I'm just selective about the reality I accept," said Bill Watterson. Many women deny the reality of what seems so obvious in abuse from these Red Flag Men. Sometimes the abuse leaves them depressed and blurs reality. Feelings of being in a deep, dark pit encompass women, render them fearful, and trap them into falsely thinking they have no way out. You always have options. You always have choices. Calling your mother, close relative, or friend is one of them. Red flags are flying the moment you feel your personal space invaded in any way.

Do you see physically abusive patterns in his family or around his friends? Do you ever have the slightest feelings of fear around this Red Flag Man? When you are with him, do things seem to be slowly but surely escalating from threatening foul language to slamming doors to cornering you and ultimately to slapping, hitting, kicking, or punching? Are you tiptoeing around to keep the peace? These obvious red flags demand your immediate attention. Fear and depression commonly take over women who can't or won't recognize physical abuse for the dangerous travesty that it is.

Has a Red Flag Man ever threatened to harm you physically or hit you, causing you to fear him? Has someone who loves you warned you of the possibility of physical abuse in your relationship? Did you listen? If not, why not? If you have been hurt in any bodily way, do you seriously believe his apology? Are his violent behaviors toward you increasing at a dangerous level in your relationship? Is your personal space respected? If you have the line drawn in your mind before such abuse ever comes up, you will be prepared to stand up for yourself. Be safe by not allowing any inappropriate physical action to be ever taken against you by a Red Flag Man.

chapter seven

He Messes with Minds

*The pain of the mind is worse than the
pain of the body.*
Publilius Syrus

An obedient, responsible, straitlaced little girl grew up in a confusing home situation. Her incompatible parents tolerated a volatile marriage because the father traveled for a living and was home only on the weekends. This firstborn child found herself continually torn between two different ideologies. Had she been able to mesh them, they could have made her well-rounded. Instead, they befuddled her, gave her continual stress and low self-esteem, and left her feeling unloved and inept.

Her mother instilled in her strict manners and morals along with amazing organizational skills. Her father encouraged her to explore, experiment, and enjoy life more. She resorted to attempting with all her heart and soul to please her mother during the week and her dad on the weekends, but she ended up pleasing no one. The hopelessness and continual dichotomy left her mind boggled and made her feel crazy.

Her unfortunate home situation left her vulnerable to a Red Flag Man who would make her feel the same way. She would have benefited from knowing more about Red Flag Men so she could have understood what was happening to her and stood up for herself. Even her mother did not understand the crazy-making chaos they all endured. Thankfully, she understands now and wants to make sure her daughters do too. She wants to begin a new and healthier way of living.

You have heard the story of the carrot being dangled in front of the donkey to get him to pull the cart, but have you ever had that carrot dangled in front of you? If you find yourself caught up in the unlikely dreams of a Red Flag Man, consider yourself warned. You might hear him say, "Someday I will finish my education and get a better job. When I make my first million, we'll have a fabulous home." Dreams are nice, but we live in reality. Accepting that and being aware of crazy-making tactics is critical in relationships.

A Red Flag Man father who was never satisfied got a kick out of taking his children to open houses in wealthy neighborhoods. He would talk as if they might live there someday, tantalizing them with unrealistic hopes and dreams. They would return home unhappy, unsatisfied, and definitely ungrateful for the nice home they did live in. The whole situation made the mother unhappy. This Red Flag Man not only confused his children but he also tormented their mother. She had to listen to the children's dissatisfaction and complaints. She appreciated the real life they had, and the recurrent, tumultuous situation her Red Flag Man created within their family drove her crazy. This unfortunate trait causes great strain in relationships and is extremely hard to understand or explain.

Dreams are nice, but we live in reality.

In the innocence of youth, a dear friend was swept off her feet following college by a tall, charming, handsome, athletic Red Flag Man. Over the years, this smart, beautiful, and talented woman underwent various unnecessary plastic surgeries at her husband's insistence, never able to satisfy him. He spoke negatively of her in groups of people, with her sitting right there. In a joking manner, he openly flirted with and made comments about women he thought were younger or more attractive. Slowly but surely, she began to feel askew because she never felt loved and appreciated for who she was. She has suffered emotionally, mentally, and physically her entire married life. If a Red Flag Man makes you feel crazy, consider the source.

In *Stop! You're Driving Me Crazy*, Dr. George R. Bach admits that there is no set list to match all possibilities and that this "driving me crazy" happens continually in various places other than intimate relationships. Different people have diverse tolerance levels and concerns.

However, this maddening annoyance becomes a huge red flag when it destroys trust and goodwill between partners.

The Red Flag Man displaying this characteristic stuns and bewilders you. Through words and actions, he throws you off balance and catches you off guard. You find yourself wishing you could get away and feeling inwardly suspicious as if something is wrong. You have a weird feeling of emptiness and ambivalence, as if you have lost yourself and your personal values. Those very feelings alert you to serious issues needing to be addressed.

Ultimately, this crazy-making treatment leads to dominance over you, leaving you feeling incapable and insane. Where do you draw the line on being teased, tolerating broken promises, hearing lie after disappointing lie, being denied thoughts of your own, and having no semblance of normal communication with your partner who supposedly loves you?

As a burglar or robber invades your property and steals your possessions, so this Red Flag Man slowly invades your right to your own feelings and your own mind. Dr. Bach calls it "mind raping." That combined with mind reading and mind ripping form a formidable triad. Slowly causing discomfort and isolation, Red Flag Men wreak havoc on typical communication and make you feel crazy.

When someone supposedly near and dear to you makes you feel insane, red flags are waving. If that thought goes through your head, heed the warning. This cruel behavior may seem enchanting and romantic at first when he says,

"I know what you are thinking and feeling." In reality, a boundary, even a line, has been irrevocably crossed and invaded. You alone have the rights to your own feelings, perceptions, and thoughts. Recognizing the slightest crazy feelings should alert you to consider the source. Talk to someone you can trust, but don't just let it go. Your mother may understand more than you can imagine.

"Who you are speaks so loudly that I can't hear what you're saying," said Ralph Waldo Emerson. You need to be smart and aware of who this Red Flag Man is and what he is doing to you. This very real mind-loss or feeling of being insane comes about gradually, indirectly, and subversively at your expense. Knowledge of this characteristic will help you be more aware of its total, encompassing nature. Take note of all the important things learned about this Red Flag Man so you can know him when you see him.

"The greatest problem in communication is the illusion that it has been accomplished," said George Bernard Shaw. The Red Flag Man will tell you and make you think you cause all the problems with the communication and the relationship. You could be told to do two opposite things and then chastised because you did only one of them. You are conditioned to jump when told to jump. You will know in uncertain terms that "it is his way or the highway." If you have suffered such an ultimatum from a Red Flag Man, consider that your own direct, personal, and very serious warning.

We often joke like Mark Twain: "Of all the things I've

lost, I miss my mind the most." However, the ramifications of experiencing this characteristic don't paint an especially appealing picture. Having undergone brain surgery, I know the loss of one's mind cannot be taken for granted. After signing pages of release forms warning of possible stroke, vegetative state, and seizures, I knew my tumor would be gone, but I wasn't sure of much else. Our minds should be guarded, treasured, and defended as part of our personal space, along with the rights to our own sanity. With a Red Flag Man, you must take charge of your own mind. Losing it to age is one thing, but losing it to a Red Flag Man is entirely another that can, and must, be avoided.

You are in charge of your life, destiny, and mind.

Kahil Gibran warns, "The reality of the other person lies not in what he reveals to you, but what he cannot reveal to you. Therefore, if you would understand him, listen to what he does not say." Pay attention. Most controlling, abusive possibilities will not magically go away by virtue of some glamorous wedding ceremony. Consider carefully the state of your mind when you are with a Red Flag Man. Momentary comfort and pleasure with him may fizzle like a sparkler on the Fourth of July. Yes, you are in charge of your life, destiny, and mind.

Be consciously aware of what is happening to your mind

when you are with a Red Flag Man. Listen to your mother if she sees it and recognizes warning signs before you do. Her years of experience and knowledge combined with her love for you enable her to add to your warnings and confirm your own fears. Don't be foolish if she hits too close to home; just take what she says to heart. Then later you will thank her for saving your sanity. Seeking counsel from a friend, therapist, or relative could serve the same purpose, but you must listen well and find your own, strong path.

Being treated respectfully as a human being extends to having your opinions, thoughts, and words respected as well. Lack of such consideration often crushes an idea because those you love, and you think love you, hold great power over you. What is said or left unsaid constitutes communication, often making us emotionally dependent on the opinions of the people we love and care about. A Red Flag Man can drive you crazy by constantly making light of your special ideas, hopes, and dreams, ultimately making you feel demeaned, worthless, insignificant, and crazy.

Remember, he acts as if everything revolves around him. You will have to look elsewhere to find warmth, support, and sincere dedication. In this crazy-making situation, only one person is truly crazy, and it is *not* you. Be alerted if this Red Flag Man's words don't jive with his actions. If he always makes suggestions about ways *you* can change or starts to make you feel out of touch with reality, he may be messing with your mind. You should be seeing red flags.

He Plays Passive-Aggressive Games

Never confuse motion with action.

Benjamin Franklin

*I*n the film *Gaslight*, Charles Boyer plays a passive-aggressive man attempting to convince his wife that she is losing her mind so he can get her into a mental institution and take her valuable family jewels. She searches for a brooch she knows she left on the dresser, but he hid it in the attic. His hounding comments make her question her own sanity. When she asks about the light from the gaslight, he retorts, "What gaslight?"

And so the frustrating ruse continues. The husband takes charge as he passively makes a way for what he aggressively desires. The mixed message occurs when he appears to care about her and her problem of losing her mind, while he causes her mental duress all along and really cares only about her inheritance. Variations of this scenario appear with Red Flag Men today. Figuring out their hidden agenda resembles going through a difficult maze. Being overcome by their passive niceties can make being aware of their negative aggressiveness difficult. Gaining knowledge of this characteristic is particularly valuable since it could easily catch you off guard.

An attractive, young teacher attended a faculty end-of-school session. "Why is everyone looking at me so funny? What is wrong?" she asked. Those words were the aggressive side attempting to cover up what she had passively been doing all year. Basically, she had missed school almost every Friday, neglecting to get a sub or leave any plans on her desk. For nine months, her team had been required to cover for her negligence and split up her class, adding to their already crowded classrooms. They were understandably upset. She neither asked what happened to her class when she was absent nor thanked the multitude of teachers who covered for her.

Acting passively, she showed no remorse for the inconvenience she had caused the other teachers and her students who missed her. Her mixed message said, "I am here today, and things are great!" Yet her aggressive actions said she liked long weekends, no matter what, and could care less about her irresponsible actions all year.

Red Flag Men often act aggressively while appearing passive. Obviously behavior presents extremely frustrating and maddening struggles as well as very complex issues in relationships. Men exhibiting this characteristic slowly frustrate you, leave tasks undone, make up excuses, and emanate an odd sense of time, often dawdling beyond anyone's limit of patience. Have you noticed any similar signs in the man you are dating? Can he tolerate losing even a child's game? These are important warnings.

In yet another peculiar situation, a Red Flag Man introduced his mistress to his wife in his office setting. He prompted the bizarre interaction between them, one woman totally oblivious and the other young, secretive, confused, jealous, and off-balance. The kind, thoughtful wife brought cards, gifts, and flowers to the mistress, thinking of her as a friend. Months would pass before the truth came out and the wife realized that was just one of the many ways she had been set up by her Red Flag Man husband.

Such humiliating craziness is only one aspect of the many confusing passive-aggressive games this Red Flag Man plays with your life and at your expense. His I-am-a-fabulous-husband attitude of putting his arm around his wife while winking and toying with his mistress wins the mixed-message-of-the-century award. Watching for signs of passive-aggressive behavior in a Red Flag Man can spare you comparable trauma. Such problematic insanity can be tricky for even a professional counselor to detect. Consider carefully listening to the voice of experience in any form available to you.

A friend's husband was pampered at work by his staff, and he expected the same treatment when he got home. My friend took care of their children all day and looked forward to her husband coming home and helping with the kids, dinner, and chores. After a while, she began to dread his homecoming. He passively dodged unpleasant responsibilities, procrastinated necessary duties, avoided confrontations, and generally acted like the father-of-the-year award belonged to him.

This Red Flag Man never really listened to his wife, conveniently forgot important activities, was often sullen, and became a belligerent tyrant when ultimately forced to communicate or take action on vital issues. This Red Flag Man acted like another child and demanded much from his wife, expecting her to do his errands and routine responsibilities.

Once again, this Red Flag Man characteristic shows up gradually and subtly, often marked by a pervasive pattern of negative attitudes. This problem manifests itself as resentment, stubbornness, sullenness, repeated failure to do tasks, and irresponsibility. Repercussions accumulate and gradually cause more discomfort and inconvenience in the relationship. If you ever feel diminished as a human being in any way due to his behavior towards you, take note and beware.

Some aptly describe him as being like a defiant teenager or a "difficult character." Things must be his way or no way, and he insists upon always being right, never at fault. No fair fights exist with a Red Flag Man. He cannot even lose a game of checkers with his own children. He makes you suffer for wanting him and promises but never delivers. With a peaceful look on his face, he withholds, humiliates, and manipulates. With his teeth gridlocked, he insists, "I am doing this because I love you!" Are you thinking that there is nothing loving about this man? This insane, emotionally torturous game spells nothing but trouble for you and your future children.

Red Flag Men need an adversary: you.

Questions abound surrounding this characteristic. Women wonder what causes such erratic, frustrating, and maddening behavior. Dr. Scott Wetzler discusses this at length in his book, *Living with the Passive-Aggressive Man.* This man lacks self-confidence and makes up for it by causing a power struggle with his partner. This trait fractures relationships because of the passivity, elusiveness, and aggressive resistance to you. Dr. Wetzler reminds us that these men need an adversary: you.

The red flags exist, and your knowledge will help you recognize them. If you are careful, you can begin to sense the mixed messages, call him out on the discrepancies, and attempt communication. Therapy may be required, but if denied, then even more red flags will crop up. These Red Flag Men possess seductive qualities that make them seem steadfast and cause you to disregard your better judgment, putting you on an ambiguous emotional seesaw. Their sins of omission cause continual disappointments. Supersensitive by nature, they cannot and will not take criticism in any shape, form, or fashion, especially from you. They tend to monopolize all your time because they just don't have many friends of their own. Does any of this sound familiar?

Consider one woman's regrettable experience with a well-seasoned, a passive-aggressive Red Flag Man: Having survived an initial divorce, she started her own successful retail business and nearly finished raising her children when a seemingly nice, wealthy man charmed her. They dated several years, and she received the overwhelming approval of those who loved her when they married. She demonstrated hope and courage to begin again in a new setting with a new man. Everything seemed to be in order. They were off to a good start, blended family and all.

They had barely gotten settled into their new life together when she had a routine checkup that detected breast cancer. This tragic news rapidly changed things. She had successful surgery. She came home, facing a long recovery that included chemotherapy, and then the first bombshell hit.

He announced that his elderly, ill mother was moving in with them for his wife to care for since he had an important business to run. Precisely at this point, the messages began to be obviously mixed. He passively showed support to his mother who needed assistance, but aggressively informed his ill wife that she, though battling cancer and undergoing chemo, would need to take care of her mother-in-law.

This strong lady met the task, exhibiting strength and

courage, fighting the cancer on top of the extra load of caring for his mother. She made the best of the tumultuous situation. Then another glitch presented itself when the cancer showed up in her lungs. This turned out to be more than he could handle. She valiantly fought for her life, desiring to finish raising her children. However, her passive-aggressive husband had an agenda of his own.

He told her to leave immediately and filed for divorce. This beautiful, smart, hard-working woman who deserved the best got booted out of her own home. Her condition quickly deteriorated as extended family cared lovingly for her. She made arrangements for her last two children, and then she died with no husband devotedly sitting by her bedside. That Red Flag Man escaped out of there faster than lightning.

Would you know this Red Flag Man if you met him? He turned out to be the opposite of all that he seemed to be. His cleverly disguised agenda fooled everyone. If asked today, in retrospect, her family could probably say that red flags existed and were overlooked or ignored.

When dating and pursuing relationships, remaining alert and observant pays off. Only you can ask, "What about me?" You are special and deserve to live your life as you desire. Prudently use this valuable knowledge to save yourself before your life is smothered or suffocated by a Red Flag Man.

This Red Flag Man gives the word "control" an entirely new connotation. He passively puts you in charge of the household, and then he aggressively greets you by saying,

"Leave all the important business to me. You ask too many questions." You are in a no-win situation if things progress to this point. Knowledge of what to look for can spare you such problems. If things don't make sense to you, delve into the reason. Trust yourself more and confirm your inner feelings by giving your mother or trusted confidante a call.

Listening to your inner voice can guide you as well. *I'll Follow the Moon*, a beautiful children's book, tells a sweet story about baby sea turtles hatching and following the moon on the sandy beaches to their safe ocean home. We as women need to use our brains and follow our souls to peace and freedom. Just as the baby sea turtles innately know to look up and follow the moon, you know in your heart of hearts what is right, just, and good to follow. You know you deserve the best. Trust yourself when things don't seem right or something bothers you.

Using your brain to its full capacity, follow your inner soul and make good choices. You can do it. Do not fall into the trap where a Red Flag Man makes you think you are the problem. No one is perfect, but you are not the problem here. If you feel fearful in any way, step back. If your opinion is not allowed or constructive criticism isn't tolerated, consider the impact of such demands. If he acts like a spoiled, teenage brat and not like a mature adult, that is a huge red flag signal for you. If you sense hidden hostility of any kind, know you and your future children will suffer greatly for it sooner or later.

If a Red Flag Man says one thing and means something

entirely different, that leaves you at a loss and destined to fail. If he acts like a poor sport and can't take losing a game, something is wrong. Forgetting obvious and important responsibilities you have asked him to do for you and your children says a lot about the value he places on his family and on your time.

Do you sense a pretense of caring?

When you are with a Red Flag Man, do you sense a pretense of caring? Are extreme demands made of you while he seems to do nothing? Does he conveniently and regularly leave the dirty work to you? Do you feel you are on the losing end of a continual, unspoken power struggle? Does he seem steadfast but act lackadaisical? Do you feel confused with his expectations and baffled by his denunciations? Does he have a negative demeanor and often seem difficult to get along with?

Only you can answer these and other critical questions honestly and carefully. Those who love and care about you may get a glimpse of the mixed messages you are experiencing. For your own peace and happiness, try to be open and objective as you listen to those who love you and care about you. Experiencing your own personal joy doesn't result from a life with a passive-aggressive Red Flag Man.

chapter nine

He Has a Cheating Heart

*Better keep yourself clean and bright.
You are the window through which you
must see the world.*

George Bernard Shaw

A delightful woman met a handsome man at a seminar. They instantly hit it off and had much in common. They decided to have dinner, and he got her cell phone number. They enjoyed each other's company and did fun things together. A few months into the new relationship, he confessed to being a married man, although "terribly unhappy" and considering separation. Naturally, he told her she really made him happy. They continued to take pleasure in their stolen moments together until she started to nag him. Their double life began showing signs of stress and guilt.

She wanted to know exactly when he planned to separate and divorce. The Red Flag Man stalled, putting the blame on his current wife. The mistress began to hate his mean, controlling wife. One day his wife learned about the affair, and that prompted him to call his mistress, sobbing and saying he loved them both. Yet he had decided to remain with his wife for the sake of their children. Several months later, he called and begged her to get involved again. Luckily she had learned her lesson, had gotten on with her life, and turned him down.

Many professional people go into certain fields in hopes of meeting someone who makes good money. The hospital is such a place. One nurse made a deal with her co-workers. She bet them she could win over a certain already married doctor before a year passed. She was attractive, conniving, and capable. They worked in close proximity all hours of the day and night, and her planned seduction conveniently happened. She had a huge diamond on her left hand before the year ended.

Obviously this cheating could not take place with Red Flag Men alone. There are obviously Red Flag Women as well. The Red Flag Man cheats for many of the same reasons he exhibits other typical behaviors. He feels special and that rules don't apply to him. He claims entitlement and usually gets what he wants, when he wants it. His desires reign paramount, and nothing else matters to him. Bound by no rules of the common majority, this Red Flag Man follows no moral or ethical values.

Start your investigation looking at the moral issues of cheating. Cheaters have a bad habit of lying. They are not always honest about being married when you meet them, and they are not honest about planning to leave their wives and children. Some women get an even bigger shock when he does finally divorce the first wife but dumps her, the mistress of many years, in order to have a fresh, even younger start. Understanding the often predictable progression cheaters follow may increase your awareness of danger signs.

Listening to what loved ones say and think will help too. If you are keeping something from them, that spells trouble. Looking through their eyes of experience could save you from a terrible mistake and allow you to recognize this Red Flag Man for yourself. Bring the truth out in the open, even if only for yourself.

One weekend, several couples went to dinner and then went over to one of the couple's apartments for dessert. While they were sitting around talking, the wife casually complained that apparently a large mouse was coming out at night and disturbing her kitchen. The guys decided to go to the store right then to buy an old-fashioned mouse trap and some cheese and then attempt to catch the culprit. Upon their return, they all jovially and carefully calculated the age-old strategy of catching an elusive mouse.

Setting the stage, they turned out the lights and set the trap near where they thought the creature was entering the kitchen. They placed the cheese on the trap and pulled back the lever. Hiding behind the bar ledge, four grown adults eagerly watched and waited silently in the dark. To their astonishment, the mouse slowly crept out from under the kitchen cabinets and then slowly proceeded to the disguised trap. True to his nature, he went for the bait as the trap loudly snapped, capturing him. They couldn't believe their eyes.

A cheating Red Flag Man can be as predictable as that mouse in the kitchen. He appears innocent and seemingly harmless. He avoids your questions as he wines and dines you. As the relationship progresses, the truth of his other life becomes harder to hide. Once he confesses he is already married, the open lying begins. He gives every excuse in the book and then falsely makes the promises you desire and demand to hear. This progression of events in a clandestine affair ends only one way, hurting everyone involved. That mouse could have sensed trouble looking at the trap or noticed eyes in the dark watching him had he been more observant. He could have resisted the cheese and found food elsewhere on his own. The same applies to you.

Checking out men you date pays off.

Checking out men you date pays off. If you think they may be married, they probably are, and that signals red flags. Upon finding out that this Red Flag Man is indeed married, ending the relationship seems like a no-brainer. Continuing, hoping for more, spells danger just like taking that cheese caused the trap to snap. Once caught, escaping without hideous consequences to everyone concerned becomes impossible.

The knowledge necessary to combat a Red Flag Man

with a cheating heart will need to be combined with all the strength and courage you can rally. We've previously spoken of lines and crossing them, but now you approach the biggest line to date. Dealing with a cheating Red Flag Man not only has you near a very fine line, but you're also left standing at the division of the road of life deciding which way to go. Are you willing to join him in becoming a cheater yourself? With other characteristics of a Red Flag Man, such as family dysfunction, obsessions with possessions, being controlled or abused by him, your choices mainly would affect you and possibly your future children if you married him. The stakes step up higher now. Many more innocent people are involved when dealing with a cheating, already married Red Flag Man who probably has children. Your critical decision may determine if you can look at yourself in the mirror every morning and live with what you have chosen to do for the rest of your life.

What about the first wives, the starter wives, of these Red Flag Men and the innocent children they brought into this world? These original families eventually pay a dreadful price through no fault of their own. Accumulating guilt can have a paralyzing effect as you compromise yourself unnecessarily for a Red Flag Man. If you find yourself in a compromising situation with a Red Flag Man, another warning sign has entered the picture.

Dr. James Dobson describes the scenario perfectly in his straightforward book, *Love Must Be Tough*. He says, "Nothing in human experience can compare with the agony of knowing that the person to whom you pledged eternal devotion has betrayed your trust." Does your clandestine affair require that you meet and date in secret and not tell a soul? That screams that what you are doing is very wrong and dangerous.

The charming lines you will inevitably hear haven't changed over the years. "My wife just doesn't understand me. We have been unhappy for ten years. We have an 'open marriage' and both date other people. I've never felt like this before. I can talk to you about anything." An additional red flag will be that he will keep you away from his family and ask you to not tell your family about the relationship. Your secret rendezvous may feel romantic at first, but what kind of future do you hope for in such a situation?

Being careful and smart deserves our attention.

In her book, *Get Rid of Him*, Joyce L. Vedral, PhD, explains that there are four ways that women get caught in the infidelity trap with a cheating Red Flag Man. The first is just a fling, meant to be a one-night stand, that leads to more. Next, you know he is married but unhappily, and you hope to marry him yourself. Third, you have no idea he is married. He wears no ring and falsely leads you on. Last, you seriously believe all the good men are taken and just go for what you can get.

A dear, beautiful friend was married to a man who said, "Women go after me more when I wear my wedding ring than when I don't." He was handsome, debonair, charming, and flirtatious. He took full advantage of all the attention he attracted from younger women. She stuck it out with him as long as she could for the sake of their children. After their divorce, he dated women the age of his oldest daughter and turned into a party animal. He still remains an accident waiting to happen for some naïve, unsuspecting woman. If you use the knowledge you are accruing, you won't fall into his snare. You will know that cheating Red Flag Man when you meet him.

Being careful and smart deserves our attention. A lovely, intelligent woman was nearing the age of thirty and very much wanted to be married and have a family. Most of her friends and sisters were already married. She did marry, and their life seemed to move along amicably for a few years. Though she missed the red flags before the marriage, she picked up on them afterwards.

He accidentally left the computer on one morning. She witnessed the porn sites he had frequented, and that led her to investigate his emails where she discovered clandestine meeting plans with another woman. She just added cheating to the long list of Red Flag Man charac-teristics. Confrontation ultimately led to separation. He refused counseling and moved in with his mistress, leav-ing his wife no choice but divorce.

You now have facts about that line, plus knowledge of what lines not to fall for. Check out a man's marital status before ever having a date with him. Even if he paints a horrific picture of his current marriage, he is still a married man. What do you think his current wife would say about him? How could you entrust you life to a man who is obviously already a cheater? What will stop him from cheating on you some future day as well?

Do you even slightly suspect he is married? Do you honestly believe he never loved his wife and the mother of his children? Are you that desperate for money and the illusion of stability? Don't you believe you deserve better than being used and hurt like that? Taking the knowledge you have been given and making wise choices while maintaining your self-respect will benefit you. You have your entire wonderful life ahead of you. Alone is much better than wasting time on the wrong, cheating Red Flag Man.

chapter ten

He Demands Center Stage

We must learn our limits. We are all something but none of us is everything.

Blaise Pascal

Jocks are notorious for strutting around campus thinking they are hot stuff. Years ago, they even got special treatment in school. One particular football player even missed his last period class every day to go work out because the teacher was a staunch football fan. She also openly gave easy A's to special players. In college, the football players were easily excused from classes and tests. This particular treatment served only to reinforce the Red Flag Man mentality. Words like "arrogant" and "self-absorbed" come to mind.

After high school football games, many girls waited out in the dark, cold parking lot for their football-player dates to stroll slowly out in their letterman jackets. Those jocks showed no concern for how long the girls waited, how cold it had been, much less how unsafe it was. These Red Flag Men felt they were worth the wait and the girls were the lucky ones.

When these attitudes develop and are reinforced when a male is young, he grows up to be a Red Flag Man. One such man had packed his van full of tents, food, and supplies and spent a great weekend with a troop of boy scouts at a lake campsite. When the weekend ended, they took down the tents and packed up the van again for the trip home. Many scouts had attended, causing an extremely long line to exit the campsite. This Red Flag Man boldly drove past the entire line of vehicles and announced at the gate that he had to leave immediately. Red Flag Men believe they deserve special treatment and have no hesitation demanding it.

The name Mohammad Ali conjures quite a picture. This infamous boxer used to gloat unashamedly, saying, "I am the greatest in the world." The inflated regard he had for himself was crystal clear. The terminology describing this characteristic has not always been so apparent. In the 1960s, no one ever told me about narcissism. We might have used the term "ego maniac," but even into the 1970s, full blown narcissistic behavior had not been labeled or understood in my crowd.

This characteristic encompasses more than an embellished sense of self. A Red Flag Man not only insists on being number one but also has a need for admiration as center stage. He loudly dominates conversations, often exaggerating points in his favor. One Red Flag Man would make his wife feel his strong muscles to meet his desperate need to be admired. Appearances and outside approval are critical for this Red Flag Man.

He exudes pretentiousness and the fantasy of success. Lacking empathy or even basic concern for others, he allows no criticism or disapproval of any kind, insisting and demanding the perfect number one status and treatment. Dealing with these exaggerated egos puts tremendous strain on relationships. "Withhold admiration from a narcissist and be disliked. Give it and be treated with indifference," said Mason Cooley, PhD. This statement illustrates the impossible lose-lose situation you have with such a Red Flag Man.

A mother glanced out the window as her daughter drove up with her fiancé for a visit. She took note as her daughter got out of the car and came to the door alone. Her fiancé seemed to be staying in the car to fix his hair in the rearview mirror for an unusually long time. When she mentioned the incident later to other daughters, she was dismissed as being negative and bothersome. Three years later, after the subsequent divorce, her children said, "Mother, you were right." This Red Flag Man turned out to be a full-blown narcissist. Just looking in the mirror can be one clue you miss but your mother or good friend picks up on. You need to listen to her concerning such blatant selfishness. Of course, it goes much deeper than that, but simple acts often signify unfathomable problems.

This Red Flag Man characteristic involves an excessive ego combined with extremely illogical sensitivities. They must maintain their flawless and even superior image at all costs. Interaction with them causes confusion and craziness.

The exaggerated sense of self held by these Red Flag Men demands admiration, continual praise, and immediate compliance. Their exploitative nature overrules and overlooks the feelings or wishes of others. Their sense of entitlement leads to the need for excessive approbation and a total lack of empathy for the needs or feelings of others. If you feel somehow left out of the entire picture, that fact alone is telling you something.

"God should make more of me. I have so many great ideas." And his wife thinks, *And He should make less of useless, no-good me.* "Every woman in this city wants me. I have it all." And his partner wonders, *If I am so "lucky," why do I feel so alone and miserable?* Have you ever heard any words like that?

A very smart, attractive woman submitted to her husband's every whim. They shared several businesses, and he scheduled her to work long hours. He often called in late and took time off. He made all the financial decisions and spent lavishly on equipment, offices, an extravagant home, and a fancy car using her credit line.

This Red Flag Man made sure she checked with him concerning every decision at work, though she graduated cum laude. He criticized and degraded her incessantly. He bragged that he was the brilliant brainpower behind the successful operations and everything hinged on him, his vision, and his prowess. She had to drive the old car, was not allowed to buy new clothes, and could not display any personal belongings in the home or have a home office in an extra bedroom.

When she showed up late in the evenings after working extended shifts and driving long distances, she cheerfully called, "I'm Home." She was greeted with him saying, "So? What's for dinner?" He continued playing video games without even giving her an upward glance. She shook her head, wondering what was going on, what she had done wrong to upset him, and why his moods seemed sour. She was exploited, tuned out, and battered. She was suffering at the hands of a full-blown, narcissistic Red Flag Man.

Narcissism is characterized by extreme self-absorption, an exaggerated sense of self-importance, and a need for attention and admiration from others. Unfortunately women see it, feel it, and yet ignore it. So what does this knowledge mean for you? Recently a childhood friend answered that question. She has been divorced for years and struggled with finances, children, and health issues. She has battled her desire to share her life with a companion against the lack of suitable, prospective mates. "This applies to me in my fifties as well as to young girls. I am facing the same problems now as I did then," she said. She explained that she had been dating a very nice man for over a year, but she added, "Everything revolves around him. He *has* to be number one and center stage. 'We' are all about him. Where he wants to eat, when he is free, his schedule, his favorite food or movie, his friends, his family, his games to watch, his dog, his car, his workout schedule, and his sleep patterns totally monopolize the relationship."

The next question my friend needs to answer is "Why

are you still dating this obvious Red Flag Man?" She temporarily exists in the picture to be dominated and manipulated for this Red Flag Man's personal purposes only. She admits to deciding to ignore, overlook, make excuses for, and tolerate the entire situation. Deep in her heart, my friend knows better and deserves so much more.

No one loves watching *Father of the Bride* more than my seven daughters and I. We love the interactions, the music, the flowers, the love, the hope, and, most of all, the happy ending. Unfortunately there will be no "cleaving unto you" with a narcissistic man. His agenda will be his own, with no regard for you or your family. Wedding vows are not serious covenants to self-centered, superior, "greatest-of-the-great," "I-am-number-one" Red Flag Men. That eliminates kindness, communication, devotion, faithfulness, and true love.

He steals all that is you.

He steals all that is you. Identity theft today is cause for concern and safety measures. Exercising the same caution protecting your identity in relationships would be wise. If you are not careful, you can be blindsided by this one-sided, manipulative, self-serving love and made to feel totally dependent, and then you begin to question how you could survive without him. At this point, you would have lost yourself. This Red Flag Man does not embezzle funds; he just steals the love out of your life, sapping your total identity in the process.

The most horrendous consequence of this and other Red Flag Man characteristics can be divorce. Living with a Red Flag Man proves extremely difficult, but surviving the aftermath is equally horrific in different ways. Unfortunate women and children left in the wake suffer endlessly and needlessly. Watching for all these warning signs is imperative.

Do you feel relief when he is gone?

These Red Flag Men expertly manipulate, twist facts, confuse, and gyrate issues beyond recognition, leaving your head spinning in disbelief. Unfortunate consequences do not have to be yours. Using the knowledge you are gaining will help you to save yourself. A new, informed generation of good, kind, caring women can be strong and turn things around by making wise choices. Taking full advantage of this educating process will allow you to maintain your dignity, stand up for yourselves, know that line when you see it, and be able to lead peaceful, happy lives. Knowing yourself well enough will enable you to use the valuable information you have to make wiser decisions.

As you assess your situation, consider answering these questions. Does he dominate most conversations, boasting about himself? Does he demand your admiration? Does he make you feel sad about yourself? Do you feel taken for granted? Finally and most importantly, do you feel you have lost your identity with him?

The strongest warning sign of a Red Flag Man is often how you are affected, influenced, and controlled when you are with him. Do you feel relief when he is gone? If you feel the least bit uneasy in his presence but can't explain why, that is your first and most important red flag warning. Take it seriously.

PART TWO

How Are You Affected When You Are with Him?

Our feelings are our most genuine path to knowledge.

Audre Lorde

chapter eleven

How Are You Affected Emotionally?

Feelings are much like waves, we can't stop them from coming, but we can choose which one to surf.

Jonatan Mårtensson

Over forty years ago, in high school, a young girl had an experience with a Red Flag Man choir director that left indelible emotional scars on her life. Her entire year in Honors Choir had led up to a choir bus trip to a nearby town. A week prior to the trip, this Red Flag Man called out the list of people going on the trip by sections. Only one name was omitted and not called, hers. All her good friends were jumping up and down with excitement, making her want to disappear. The only explanation was that there were forty-two seats on the bus, and she somehow ended up being the unlucky forty-third.

Her feelings were hurt and her teenage emotions devastated. She had practiced hard, made good grades, attended every early rehearsal, and harmonized well. She will never know why she was cut, but she will always remember how she felt. Red Flag Men negatively affect women emotionally.

Being with them can influence how you feel, act, and are influenced by and respond to control.

Looking back, the girl could have scheduled an appointment with him to get an explanation and let him know how what he had done made her feel. Not all emotional issues in your life will be that clear, but they all deserve your undivided attention. You often put up with things in your life by ignoring their significance and letting them go on too long. You procrastinate taking appropriate action to care for yourself.

One girl graduated from college, worked retail for years, and then landed a job combining her retail skills with her communications degree. She loved going to work until they hired a new Red Flag Man store manager. She immediately sensed an attitude about him and felt he treated her in a demeaning way. "Get that trash out of here," he would say. He had that pampered, spoiled-brat air about him. She began documenting his statements and behavior, and then she went to her boss with the evidence. She took a stand and refused to be treated disrespectfully at her job. This one man made her feel depressed and hate the job she once loved. She had options and used them. Luckily she saw the truth about this Red Flag Man immediately. That is not always the case.

Remember the old story of the frog that plops happily into a pot of slowly heating water? He hops and swims jubilantly, unaware of the burner being turned on high. Slowly but surely over time, the water warms, then reaches a full, rolling boil that eventually scalds the frog who meets his demise, cooking in the same water he joyfully played in earlier. He simply neglected to pay attention to what was going on in his life.

When beginning a relationship with a Red Flag Man, you may feel joyously happy at first, exactly like that frog. You may choose to ignore those characteristics you learned about or just be blissfully ignorant like the frog as the temperature was turned up. You may decide to go on despite the dangerous hot water warning you to get out. Being aware of how you feel emotionally with a Red Flag Man will help you think more clearly and make wiser choices. Emotions in relationships are much harder to decipher than a frog in boiling-hot water.

Being in a Red Flag Man relationship makes recognizing how you feel emotionally complex at first. His mesmerizing charm clouds your judgment, and yet your knowledge can return you to reality, allowing you to realize how you feel emotionally with him. Friends and family can help and support you if you allow that, but the critical choices must come from you. The frog wasn't so lucky, ignoring signs of danger. What about you? Can you make examining your emotions when you are with a Red Flag Man a priority?

Emotions or strong feelings basically consist of being sad, mad, glad, scared, and excited. Endless other emotions spring from those fundamental five which help us make decisions, communicate with others, set boundaries, and literally survive. A myriad of these emotions affect you daily along with the need to feel accepted, respected, and valued. When your emotional needs are being satisfied, you feel loved, empowered, satisfied, calm, happy, exuberant, excited, and fascinated.

On the other hand, when your emotional needs are not being satisfied, you feel anxious, frazzled, and wistful. You might also notice that you begin to feel insecure, self-conscious, or angry. If you find yourself feeling dread, despair, or foreboding, then you could be in an unhealthy relationship. Being alert and knowledgeable will enable you to decipher these dangerous and harmful emotional feelings that surface especially when you are with a Red Flag Man. Such an impressive list suggests reason enough to be vigilant, staying in touch with your emotional feelings and discovering for yourself how you feel when you are with a Red Flag Man.

An event planner excitedly coordinated her first big meeting, from the location to the food, decorations, and keynote speaker. She had everything ready and appropriately confirmed. Things went smoothly the day of the event until she noticed the speaker had not shown up early, as advised. She got busy with other details and did not consider the problem again until the tables filled up and it was time to begin.

Starting to sweat, she hurriedly found her notebook and began calling all the numbers she had on file for the speaker. He was unreachable. Feeling extremely stressed, she finally realized she would have to cover for him, which she was not adequately prepared to do. She learned some important lessons that day. You too have many lessons to learn about The Red Flag man and how you are affected emotionally when you are involved with him.

She never heard from the speaker and later learned he was notorious for overbooking and not calling or caring. This obvious Red Flag Man had no remorse about disappointing a crowd of people or causing her emotional trauma. If you find yourself suffering such unnecessary disappointments in your relationship with a Red Flag Man, consider yourself warned. Why set yourself up to be let down, frazzled, and tormented with negative feelings?

A Red Flag Man has no problem hurting your feelings, and some of these negative feelings affect your life choices and remain with you forever. *First Wives Club*, a television mini-series, revealed the trauma of women who had been hurt emotionally by Red Flag Men. But the women eventually enjoyed revenge on the Red Flag Men who hurt them.

In one episode, the Red Flag Man had ignored his lovely wife because of his obsession with his prized show car. His not being there for her emotionally left her feeling lonely, depleted, and irritated. The *First Wives Club* show bought one of his most prized cars and arranged a surprise for her. They took her up in a transport plane. She expressed supreme satisfaction about being able to push that car out of that transport plane and watch it go up in flames in the Arizona desert below. Even so, she has a damaged heart along with many other adverse side effects from years of neglectful, harmful emotional treatment.

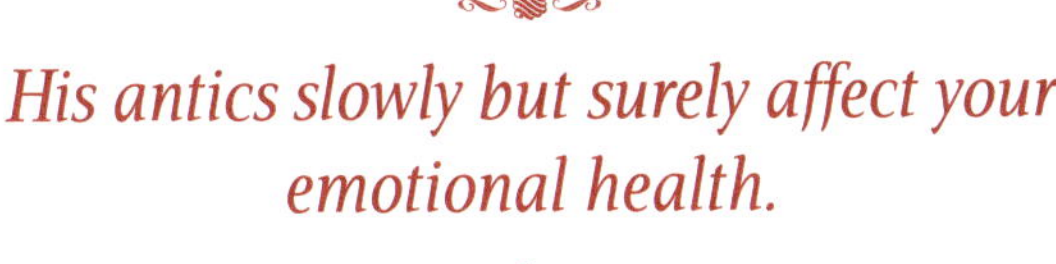

His antics slowly but surely affect your emotional health.

An emotionally healthy person controls his thoughts, feelings, and behavior. A "Dear Abby" column recently addressed emotional health. The person writing stated that Internet dating services listed only "emotionally healthy" people would be considered for dating. The writer had been treated for depression and felt like damaged goods. The reply was positive, recognizing that having a problem and getting help is better and more emotionally healthy than someone who is afraid to recognize her problems.

Red Flag Men prove to be the antithesis of emotional health, which will definitely add to your baggage load and will unfortunately spill over from the relationship onto you. His behaviors exhibit a lack of warmth, causing him to engage in continual put-downs that totally negate your individuality. His antics slowly but surely affect your emotional health.

Life with a multifaceted Red Flag Man makes you feel emotionally cold. I was swimming early one winter recently at a nearby YMCA where the water levels were down, and the morning lifeguards had to fill the pool to the top. Unfortunately, the ice-cold water poured right into my lane. In the past, they had the ice-cold water on for only a short time, but this particular morning, it ran for twenty-five minutes. The first few laps were tolerable, but then the cold water started seeping further and further down to the middle point of the lane

Life with a Red Flag Man can be just as cold as that swimming pool on that winter morning. The chill from such an experience can linger. And just like the swimming-pool incident, it happens very gradually, but before you know it, you are frozen in more ways than one. Swimming laps in that ice-cold pool ruined my day. Feeling emotionally ice-cold in a relationship with a Red Flag Man can ruin your life.

The treatment you get from a Red Flag Man taints and freezes your being. Such a combination of lack of warmth, words, and loving looks slowly but surely destroys all that is you. A Red Flag Man struggles to express warm, tender, loving, supportive, kind, or affectionate emotional feelings sincerely. In reality, he is incapable of honestly doing so for a sustained period, leaving you emotionally deprived. You can tell when words are spoken that are not from the heart. Why would you allow yourself to be frozen in a cold, meaningless relationship? Consider carefully such emotional feelings as very real warnings.

How much is finally enough? Where do you draw the line? Swimming in an ice-cold pool in the middle of winter is uncomfortable. It did not have to happen. The staff could have filled the pool the evening before but chose not to or did not think about it. I finally just got out and went home. Will you have the courage and strength to get out of the cold, honestly analyze your situation, and draw the line, ending negative emotional torture or deprivation? If you fail to do so, you will be a prisoner in your own home under the spell of a Red Flag Man.

What images come to your mind when you hear the word "prisoner"? We usually think of incarceration as being involuntarily behind bars. Women imprisoned by Red Flag Men give up their freedoms voluntarily, if unintentionally, and are kept under emotional restraint. If you give up any of your freedoms, such as expressing your opinions, making your own decisions, and fully participating in planning, you barely exist in prison-like conditions with a Red Flag Man.

Being around a Red Flag Man makes you feel like an emotional prisoner in your own home, creating a self-imposed sentence. One lady lives like a prisoner with her Red Flag Man husband and doesn't even know it. Because she stays, she must feel sentenced or somehow deserving of such a life, or she just might not know any better. She cannot go anywhere nor do anything without his permission. He controls all the funds and business transactions and keeps her on a strict budget, despite the fact that she brings home a paycheck. Like a prisoner, her decisions are all made for her. Her Red Flag Man chooses what car she drives and where she goes to get the gas to fill it. All the dirty work is left up to her, and the house has to be perfect whenever he comes home.

Beyond having any feelings of her own, she lacks feelings of appreciation, freedom, peace, and warmth. Instead, her days and nights are full of fear, aloofness, anxiety, and exhaustion. Noticing and experiencing prolonged anger, sadness, or fear in your emotional life tells you something is wrong.

No family is perfect, but when a selfish, demanding, overbearing, and demeaning Red Flag Man shows up, emotional problems cannot help but surface. If you feel like a prisoner in even a tiny way, red flags are attempting to warn you. Do you live in emotional fear of displeasing him or of his wrath being unleashed on you? Are you willing to use your knowledge to secure your own, good emotional health?

You might have lost the freedom of expressing your opinions or making personal choices, causing you to feel worthless and discouraged. Remember, the Red Flag Man acts as if his opinions matter most and he ranks number one. Women in these suppressed, emotional prison-like situations don't even realize how much they have lost or covered up. Eventually, nothing is left of you. You will have lost all your self-esteem, leaving you unable to function on your own. You are learning how it feels and how you are affected emotionally to be with a Red Flag Man.

Because the Red Flag Man makes you feel incompetent to do even simple things, your environment resembles a prison, making escape seem impossible. He thrives on your being totally dependent upon him. Pay attention to the emotions your feelings bring out in your life and then consider freedom, freedom from feeling as if you are a prisoner of a Red Flag Man. Feeling respected, accepted, and important signifies a positive, emotionally healthy atmosphere, certainly not that of a prison.

Some things are worth waiting for. I know all about waiting. I was pregnant ten times, and nine of the deliveries were late. Number five was seventeen days late, in the middle of a record heat wave in Dallas. The total of ninety plus months of being pregnant was worth the wait because the joy outweighed the pain. That waiting, though difficult, held the promise of a new baby to love and cherish. Time matters, and time is important. Being kept waiting by a Red Flag Man causes trouble, plays havoc with your emotions, and yields no promise. The subsequent negative emotions affect how you feel and how you act.

Observing people who are waiting reveals they are not very happy about it. My flight attendant friend has told me many interesting tales of passengers upset about having to wait. When flights are cancelled, long lines taking hours to reschedule mess up people's plans and tempers flare. You could describe the passengers as annoyed, furious, bored, frustrated, unhappy, and worried. These same emotional feelings cause distress and conflict in relationships. Being kept waiting endless times escalates to a crazy-making process that puts a tremendous strain on Red Flag Man relationships.

Author Eric Hoffer reminds us of this, explaining, "Rudeness is the weak man's imitation of strength." Red Flag Men exhibit rudeness, showing a lack of respect to you by being habitually late and making you wait. Being kept waiting makes you feel emotionally distraught and sends the message that his time is more valuable than yours.

Punctuality relates to honesty, respect, and kindness. A Red Flag Man who cares about only himself and operates on his own standard time makes everyone in contact with him miserable. Dishonesty about being somewhere when he says he will be, warns you that he won't be honest about other things in the relationship. He is the one being dishonest and late, but somehow he turns things around, making you feeling guilty, resentful, and disappointed. His attitude works for him but not for you.

If your emotional feelings are troubling you, talk to someone you trust or seek counseling from someone you trust. Those who love and care about you may have noticed changes in your emotional state and let you know of their desire to help. That help is often a phone call away, no questions asked. You make a choice to risk becoming an emotional wreck over a Red Flag Man. You can make a choice to seek help, too.

We women bear the brunt of statements concerning our tender emotions. We cringe to hear a man say, "She's just hysterical, over nothing." A woman airline passenger wrote a book communicating her hysterical terrorist-like experience on a flight to California. For a long time, her alarm and concern met with resistance. Facts, documents, and concurrent eyewitness accounts have now proven her concerns worthy of attention and respect. Her book tells the entire frightening story for the world to read. Women suffering from conflicting emotional issues with Red Flag Men have very similar problems, not only in being heard but also in being taken seriously.

One such woman was vulnerable and on shaky ground from the beginning of her Red Flag Man relationship. She married him against the wishes of her parents. Walking down the aisle, she felt ready and prepared to handle her marriage, and she felt happy and confident in their future together as a couple.

The initial emotionally frustrating game concerned time. She was kept waiting in every situation, leaving her confused and irritated. Her Red Flag Man never listened to her when she tried to discuss her concerns with him. Overcome with his gloating self-importance and demeaning attitude of what she did, she felt incompetent about everything. Already having alienated and detached her from close family, this Red Flag Man had her all to himself.

She grew self-conscious about everything she did, fearing his teasing and harsh judgment. She retreated like a turtle into its shell, insecure and afraid. She felt trapped and dismayed, and yet she rationalized his behavior as related to stress or health reasons. Her demanding Red Flag Man totally depleted her of her natural exuberance and positive outlook. She resorted simply to trying to get through the days, hoping for better ones ahead. She suffered emotional deprivation from lack of being able to communicate and interact positively with her Red Flag Man.

Having children gave her a short respite, but soon that only complicated the emotional roller coaster she rode with this Red Flag Man. He resented her time with the children and began making even more demands than before, leaving her emotionally drained and hopeless at times. With only so many hours in the day and only so much of her to go around, she felt exasperated.

Before long, she felt dread and foreboding in his presence as well as lonely, though surrounded by her family. She struggled with the simplest of daily tasks. She mastered well the art of faking in front of everyone. She lacked any warmth or tenderness in her daily existence. Finally fate intervened to spare her a full-blown emotional breakdown by ushering in improved, though painful, life changes. Years of therapy and the passing of time finally eased her load, helped her understand what she had endured, and ultimately gave her a beautiful second chance at life. All those years lost to her could have been different had she known more clearly what was happening.

Having knowledge about how being with a Red Flag Man can make you feel will be an invaluable aid in detecting such symptoms. Emotions are serious things. A car just doesn't break down all of a sudden. You have warning signs, close calls, and numerous quick fixes until finally it has to be towed and repaired in order to run. Eventually the facts must be faced and the bills paid. If you are with someone claiming to love you, you should feel good and comfortable but not lost, fearful, stranded, or lonely. Those emotional signals are warnings to you so that you can remedy the situation before breaking down.

Consider your personal emotional baseline. Years ago my doctor ordered a bone density scan to serve as a baseline for use in later years when my bones start changing with age. She has used this report many times to compare my bone mass and get me started on bone strengthening medications to avoid osteoporosis. Without the original baseline graph, my doctor could not distinguish changes in my bones. Correspondingly we need an emotional baseline to compare our feelings when we are happiest to when things change to unhappy or miserable.

Happy times can and should be the norm. However, keeping a sustained happy-time scenario going seems to be not only rare but challenging these days. A special example comes to mind of my happy baseline. Having experienced ten senior-class years with ten children certainly taught me a lot. Some parents say if their teenagers didn't act out so much that last year of high school, it would be impossible ever to let them go. Still the strain for independence and thinking they know it all puts considerable stress on the entire family. The senior year of my ninth child took an unexpected turn for the better.

This beautiful, talented daughter all of sudden saw her mother with new eyes full of appreciation, love, and kindness. She became cooperative, helpful, supportive, respectful, and fun. She spoke lovingly and kindly to me and enjoyed going to the grocery store, on errands, and cooking with me. It proved to be a mother's dream come true. She shared her life with me, and it turned out to be the senior year to top them all and a baseline for me of what happy can and should feel like. Of course, adult relationships are different, but my experience with my daughter shows how to determine your happy, emotional baseline.

Now you will have something to refer to and compare. Sometimes you don't realize how much a relationship has degenerated until it resolves and gets better. You've seen evidence of the warning signs of emotional instability. A day at the spa just doesn't fix such deep rooted emotional trauma. When I was growing up, my best friend's mother had to be hospitalized to begin repairing the emotional situation she could no longer ignore. Her situation finally demanded action, and yet it could have been prevented had it not been allowed to reach that dangerous point.

A nervous breakdown can occur from being overloaded with stress. Such a breakdown can manifest itself as an inability or struggle to function in normal activities or the depressive version which leads to more dramatic symptoms of uncontrollable crying, disorientation, or confusion. These breakdowns are further related to anxiety disorders or panic attacks and can disrupt daytime performance and sleep patterns at night. About one-third of Americans have felt on the verge of such a nervous breakdown at some time in their lives. Your understanding can prevent a nervous breakdown and lead to better choices and outcomes.

Your knowledge in this area can serve as a thermometer to recognize positive and negative emotions in a Red Flag Man. Help and advice from someone who cares can supplement that knowledge. Your mother or good friend may see a red flag you are missing. Tolerating emotional trauma can't help but eventually take its toll on you. Think long, hard, and seriously about all the emotional feelings churning inside of you and how they make you feel.

Taking charge of your life can prevent you from ending up shocked, devastated, and close to an emotional breakdown. Why waste valuable time and energy on a relationship draining you emotionally? Heed the warnings of those red flags. You have choices. You can draw that line and hold to it. You have knowledge, and you are not color blind; you can recognize red when you see it. Once you take control of your life, you can enjoy whatever life you choose, whether it be in helping others, cherishing friends, doing what you love, or just being yourself. You understand that not whom you are with, but who you are, that defines you and the meaning of your life.

Be thankful for friends who seem to meet their soul mate and sail off into the sunset of marital bliss. But remember, circumstances are rarely as they seem. One of my friends appeared to have the absolute perfect life. But something was making her terribly sad. She had been controlled and abused to the point of nothingness. I did not know until later that she felt like a failure, incapable of doing anything worthwhile. As she was being put down, the Red Flag Man was building up his weak and insecure ego at her expense.

Not whom you are with, but who you are, defines you.

Wake up and be aware of your true emotional feelings. Your personal life will be much more emotionally sound if you take charge of your emotional feelings. Life in general may not be fair, but it can still be wonderful, meaningful, and great. Women today have to deal with a job, husband, children, mortgage, bills, traffic, and crowded schedules. If you feel emotionally drained, and the main cause is the feelings associated with a Red Flag Man, recognizing that is the beginning of your feeling better emotionally and in every other way.

Beware if you feel dread or despair. Think seriously if you are anxious, frazzled, wistful, or emotionally depleted. Wake up to the truth of when someone asks you how you feel and you would truthfully like to say, "I am an emotional wreck." If you feel you have lost your freedoms or are kept waiting continually, you may already be on your way to feeling emotionally drained or having an emotional breakdown.

Think back to your emotional baseline and assess where you are emotionally now, compared to your ideal emotional state. Use what you have learned to make wise choices to find your way back to safe emotional constancy. You deserve emotional stability, and only you can know where your personal line needs to be drawn.

Do you feel happy or sad, comfortable or ill-at-ease with this Red Flag Man? Does he often hurt your feelings intentionally or unintentionally? Do you feel trapped or suppressed in any way? Have you voluntarily given up any of your personal rights? Does discussing things get you nowhere? Do you feel on the brink of a breakdown? Do you find yourself hiding how you really feel and what is going on from those who really love and care about you? Answering these questions honestly can open your eyes to the truth and then allow you to make wise decisions and choices.

As you continue learning, you will gain even more knowledge which can help you know where to draw that line as you make critical choices. Using that knowledge prudently can lead to significant personal choices concerning the Red Flag Man. As you learn and make wiser choices, you will be discovering him, realizing how you are affected when you are with him, and taking charge of your own life.

How Are You Affected Mentally?

One's dignity may be assaulted, vandalized and cruelly mocked, but it cannot be taken away unless it is surrendered.

Morton Kondrake

One of my daughters took a car to college in another state. While there, she had the oil changed but did not have the time, money, or knowledge about regular car upkeep to do much else. Luckily the car resembled that Eveready battery and kept on going through college and grad school. But as she and her husband were driving across the country to relocate, her car broke down on the highway. Luckily his family was following them, and she got the car repaired. How we feel mentally with a Red Flag Man can be like that car. If you do not personally guard and take care of your mental health, you can go on only so long before a negative situation results in a gradual mental breakdown.

One woman unknowingly married a Red Flag Man who used several subversive mental tactics to control her, causing her to question her mental sanity before she finally divorced him years later. The mental abuse began with his making jokes at her expense, isolating her from friends and family, and blaming her for everything wrong in their relationship. These behaviors left her feeling insecure, less vibrant, and confused. He ordered her around and exerted undue power over her.

She felt the effects of this mental tormenting for years after her divorce. Mental abuse can do irreparable damage. When you question your sanity, you are being mentally abused and need to seek help.

You need to ask, "Where do I draw the line?"

We often hear a woman say, "But he wasn't like that before we got married." The signs were probably there, but you missed them. A recent headline in the newspaper for the movie *Nancy Drew* read "Clued In." That is exactly what you need to be when dealing with a Red Flag Man and assessing how you feel mentally when you are with him. Unpleasant surprises await you with him, and your life just does not turn out as you expected.

When Krispy Kreme doughnuts finally opened a store in Dallas, cars lined the street to be there for the grand opening. What a celebration. The staff even came out to the drive-through line to give away free hot doughnuts, and they always gave away a free one inside the store. After the first few months, customers got in the mindset of expecting good service and a free, hot donut while waiting in line. Perhaps advertising is one mind game after another.

As soon as business got going and they became well established, the perks stopped. First they cut the free doughnuts in the outside line, and then they cancelled the ones inside. What a big disappointment to customers. Similarly, a Red Flag Man can keep up a front just so long before settling into unhealthy behavior patterns that make you feel mentally unstable. You need to ask, "Where do I draw the line?" If you have noticed such drastic changes in your relationship, what are you doing about it? Where is your line?

A nail technician friend knew where to draw that line. She had a predetermined limit set in her own mind concerning men she would date. Compromising and making an effort to get along is one thing, but tolerating control, manipulation, and intimidation proves quite another. Luckily she had a strong foundation of self-confidence that led her to demand being treated respectfully with no mind games allowed.

When her boyfriend started messing with her mind and mental sanity, she showed him the door. When her Red Flag Man blamed her, she didn't buy it. When he had convenient amnesia, pretending to forget important things he told her he would do, she didn't accept it. She knew what he had promised and held him to it. She had the inner strength to say, "Yes, I can make it on my own. Just watch me!" When she recognized he did not appreciate her unique qualities, quirks and all, she did not give him a second chance. She had no reason to apologize for who she was and what she stood for. When he treated her more tough than tender, she said, "Thanks, but no thanks." She refused to tiptoe or walk on eggshells. Her confidence and satisfaction with herself helped her be strong, maintain her self-esteem, get away from that Red Flag Man, and move on with her happy life. Solutions may vary, but a strong foundation will benefit you throughout your life, married or single.

Another bright, sharp woman lacked the strength and knowledge to set necessary boundaries. Unfortunately, she got mixed up with a very controlling Red Flag Man because she did not possess that very necessary strong base of self-esteem. She silently took whatever he dished out. After their marriage, he laid down the law that he would take care of all the finances and keep all records, checks, and bills under lock and key. She had to account for every penny of the minimal allowance he allotted her. Continual intimidation made her feel mentally incompetent, unsure of her abilities, and fearful.

Communication between them did not exist. If she attempted to discuss or express concerns, she was ignored, accused of causing trouble, and labeled ungrateful. He refused to listen to or acknowledge her feelings. Being made to feel totally dependent rendered her depressed and helpless to do anything about it. Her self-esteem and self-confidence eroded like the coastline at the beach. She felt mentally manipulated and run over by a Red Flag Man.

Mental abuse demolishes your self-esteem if you allow it to continue. Having confidence, proper respect, independence, and satisfaction in one's self is a basic human need. Positive self-esteem is a major key to your happiness and success. We need not only to feel respect from others but also to have it for ourselves. This knowledge will assist you in evaluating the state of your self-esteem when you are with a Red Flag Man. If how you feel about yourself starts a downward spiral, your resultant unhealthy mental state and relationship could destroy you in time. When you suffer a noticeable loss of your sense of well-being, self-esteem, self-confidence, or zest for life, you need to recognize that such feelings signal trouble. Once you realize you don't feel quite normal, you should carefully monitor your feelings.

Our mental health involves how we think, feel, and act as we cope with our individual life situations. Normally people feel worried, anxious, sad, or stressed at times. Concerns arise when those mental feelings become more severe and start to interfere with your ability to function in daily life. When you suffer a loss of your sense of well-being, self-esteem, self-confidence, or zest for life, you need to recognize that these mental feelings signal trouble. Once you are aware, it is time for you to watch your feelings or even get help from a therapist.

Mental issues can be caused by the environment, loss, illness, or life trauma. Life trauma brings the Red Flag Man into the picture. Trauma is a behavioral state resulting from severe emotional or mental stress. A traumatic state involves being emotionally tortured and then allowing your mental state to be compromised. So how do you react mentally when you are with a Red Flag Man?

How the red flag man affects you mentally happens slowly and deceptively over time. Basically your mind is messed with, and you begin to think things the Red Flag Man tells you to think. This brainwashing causes you to believe him over yourself. An unheard bell rings, and the mind games have just begun. This is one of the first ways the Red Flag Man affects your mental feelings. Telling you what to think is an unacceptable invasion of your basic human right to think for yourself.

Mind games are just one way your mind is messed with by a Red Flag Man. This shrewd process of confusing and intimidating you works deviously to the abuser's advantage. Your own good judgment gets swallowed up by his accusations. This toying with your mind continues as he repeatedly refuses to hear you out or listen to how you feel. Unquestionable mental abuse has effortlessly begun by a Red Flag Man with you as his victim.

In controlling your mind, he denies any accusations or insists you made a big deal out of nothing. Intimidation goes along with the Red Flag Man as he forces you to conform to his mold. The sad truth is that no matter what you do, give up, compromise, or attempt, it will never be enough to satisfy the Red Flag Man or keep him from causing you further confusion and mental anguish. As a victim of mind games, you struggle to understand the impact of what is happening to you. Your mind has most definitely been criminally invaded, whether consciously or subconsciously, by a Red Flag Man who makes you wonder if you are losing your mind.

Visualize the ancient scenario of a little cat cornered by a huge, angry dog. Women have described this same boxed-in feeling that evolves from being dominated, isolated, and pushed into a corner and kept there by a Red Flag Man. As a child, everyone played hide-and-seek. My children especially enjoyed playing inside on a rainy day. They found inventive places to squeeze in and hide, such as cabinets, closet shelves, laundry baskets, under beds, and in between furniture. Eventually everyone was found, and the game started over again.

Having penetrated your most tender emotions, this Red Flag Man delves into your mental state. This feels like hiding in a house, then in a room, next a closet, and finally a small box. Think of being in the tiniest, most inner part of nesting dolls. This Red Flag Man hide-and-seek-game does not end, and you are never found.

This box keeps you in your place, where he controls everything and limits your activity in the outside world. After hearing all your faults straight from his mouth, you feel strange, but you still start to believe him. This forced dependence has rendered you insecure. Escaping from this tight box seems impossible, and the longer you stay, the harder the getaway becomes. Keeping tabs on progressing relationships and having knowledge of danger signs can prevent such circumstances. A headline on a newspaper advertisement read, "Options mean you aren't fenced in." Allowing things to escalate to the point of no return sometimes makes options seem slim. Having the necessary knowledge, wisdom, and strength to realize options do exist, and then taking appropriate action, requires courage. If you don't stand up for yourself, you risk having your mind invaded, an intrusion comparable to rape.

Certain women from unstable, broken homes or those struggling with insecurities seem more susceptible to taking comfort from Red Flag Men who appear self-assured and powerful. These Red Flag Men are players of another league. They are determined and do not give up easily. At first their attention appears flattering, but it is a danger sign. Attracted to his self-assurance and coolness, unsuspecting women can fall readily for all his lines.

Having been emotionally drained, you are an easier target for mind raping from a Red Flag Man who makes you think you cannot exist without him. He quickly takes over, saying, "I do the thinking around here." Thus your mind is cut off, and the mind raping has only just begun. Another line has just been crossed. You don't lose your virginity in this rape; you potentially lose your mind.

Just as a licensed childbirth instructor cannot truly know the trauma, pain, and stress of childbirth unless she has herself given birth, a person cannot fathom mind rape unless she has been its victim. Yet being *aware* of this travesty can benefit women. A national organization offering information about women and rape warns that one in three women worldwide is at risk of being raped in the traditional sense. Statistics for mind rape are immeasurable.

Mothers warn their daughters at young ages of the dangers of rape. Women today try to protect themselves from rape by locking their doors, not walking alone in dark areas, being aware of their surroundings, not leaving their drink unattended to avoid the date rape drug, and watching out for each other. Rapists go for the core of their victims' bodies. Red Flag Men go for the core of their victims' minds. Knowledge can protect you from another rape, just as invasive and painful. The seriousness of how you are affected mentally with a Red Flag Man warrants the term "mind rape."

We know rape is a violent, hostile act, hurting, humiliating, and dehumanizing the innocent victim. This invasion is a frightening experience that can happen to anyone at any age. As a woman, young or old, dealing with a Red Flag Man, mind rape proves of equal concern. This ongoing, appalling occurrence involves invading, pillaging, and usurping your mind. Unfortunately, after a mind raping, neither a DNA sample nor visual proof of the crime can be collected. This criminal behavior interferes with another human being's mind. How do you explain that someone has altered your thinking? You are like a sufferer of Stockholm Syndrome, having been brainwashed and reprogrammed to identify with your "kidnapper," who in this case is a Red Flag Man. With no visible scars, the only tearing and bruising is on your heart. This kind of rape deserves the same attention and warning to all women. This travesty ravages its innocent victims for years, leaving them with lifelong mental scars.

Such an unfortunate scenario painfully unfolded before my very eyes with an acquaintance. This particular Red Flag Man verbally assaulted this highly educated, successful woman into thinking she was incompetent. Leaving her out of all decision-making, he managed everything his way and had total control of her. He proceeded with his own agenda at her expense. Threatening her, he forced her to do things she was uncomfortable doing and made her feel guilty if she didn't.

An optimist at heart, she hoped things would improve some day. She wondered if she could do something better or differently to please him or earn his respect and admiration. He alienated her from her family, falsely convincing her that they were against her and all she really needed was him. Her brain felt like a scrambled mass of confusion and chaos. Having had her mind raped, she felt alone and afraid. The adverse effects of being with her Red Flag Man seemed to multiply.

Having been dominated, isolated, controlled, and conditioned, she merely functioned as his puppet. The way she felt mentally with her Red Flag Man did not paint a pretty picture. She failed to realize the intense level of pain, frustration, anguish, and insanity she had silently endured until, luckily for her, fate intervened. He left.

Something similar happened to a good friend's daughter in her new marriage. Her husband has taken over her mind. He has alienated her from family and friends who would help her. Her mother is distraught at never being able to communicate with her and has resorted to writing letters and mailing them to her work. He wants her all to himself. He controls when and if she can even talk to any of her family by checking phone records. He even remains beside her when she is allowed to make phone calls.

With a Red Flag Man, you will feel invisible.

He misconstrued control for love and dominance for duty. He basically tells her what to do and think, and she obeys. She graduated from college, and yet she somehow got caught in this terrible mental trap, where she gave up all that she was for all he said. She feels fearful, blue, scared, and unhappy, and she blames herself for her plight. He continually says, "You'll never be able to 'make it' without me." The unspoken, underlying threat screams, "And you better not ever try!" Love is not about threats and control, and red flags are flying if such a scenario exists. You are wonderful and strong, and you can make it on your own if necessary. You also deserve to be lovingly and respectfully acknowledged as a human being. However, with a Red Flag Man, you will often feel invisible.

As I strolled alone along the beach of Sanibel Island early one summer morning, I noticed an incredible rainbow in one portion of the sky. In my delight and enthusiasm, I wanted to tell everyone I passed along the shore, saying, "Look up at that magnificent rainbow! Look what you are missing!" Many people were walking or jogging and totally unaware of the miracle in the sky. They proceeded as if nothing special was going on that morning. Such an instance exemplifies exactly how you may feel mentally with a Red Flag Man. You will feel like a shining and wonderful person, but at the same time you are invisible, ignored, and meaningless. These are some of the most horrible feelings in the world, especially when you are supposedly with someone who says, "I love you." Under such circumstances, your enthusiasm will melt like a popsicle on a hot summer day.

In the movie *Nancy Drew*, Nancy commented that she just couldn't give up sleuthing no matter how hard she tried. Her boyfriend aptly replied, "I guess that's just how you are, and that's okay." That important fact applies to you, and you do yourself a disservice by allowing any Red Flag Man to make you feel otherwise. He will try. In loving, healthy relationships, people that respect and care about each other acknowledge one another. Things like cheerful greetings, recognition of personal accomplishments, expressing gratitude and appreciation, and a general concern for one another's welfare should exist.

Being ignored or treated as if you are invisible, constitutes abusive and intolerable behavior that initially hurts emotionally and then mentally. If you want to disappear in your own home or find yourself retreating to a corner, be aware that things have gotten out of control. Constant exploitation causes your mental state to degenerate. Being noticed, appreciated, respected, and acknowledged are basic human needs. Blending into the woodwork as an invisible nothing occurs as a result of the mentally destructive behavior of a Red Flag Man, leaving multiple discrepancies between what should be and what is. Only you can know if your situation has reached that point. Analyzing how a Red Flag Man makes you feel mentally should be at the top of your priority list.

Educated, well-mannered, multi-talented women who are pillars of their communities, from every walk of life and every age group, all find themselves mentally distraught with Red Flag Men. When the mental games begin, they lack sufficient emotional savvy to pick up on what is happening. Soon their self-doubt overcomes them, they feel invisible, and they become mental wrecks.

Everyone remembers high school days. Boys and girls bore different burdens and yet struggled just the same. One of the worst things that went on, and probably still does, was the back-biting wars between girls fighting over certain boys. Someone would be your very best friend to your face and then turn on you in a split second. Such scenarios were mean, dirty, and hurtful. Luckily, a few good friends stuck by you, making survival possible and bearable. The same applies to you now. You have true, caring friends who want the best for you and are willing to help you out from under the Red Flag Man mental spell.

Red Flag Men do not outgrow this high school mentality of hurting you behind your back. This mentally damaging trick can cause further confusion and chaos, leaving you even more clueless and vulnerable. Once again, women are oblivious to his hidden agenda. One Red Flag Man extended the mind games with his wife. Behind her back, he went to the elementary school where his children attended classes and where she volunteered extensively and set her up for further mind games.

He told the staff that his wife was not well and that he would be handling all future school issues. He further stipulated not to involve her in any way or return her phone calls or notes. He gave an academy-award performance, totally convincing all there. She had no idea what he had done. He had mentally manipulated her for years, but he had stepped it up a level by going to the school. A Red Flag Men doesn't stop at mentally ravaging you. By painting a false picture against you, he attempts to gain allies in the community, confirming your supposed mental state, ironically created by that Red Flag Man.

Years after his school visit, a kind staff member informed her of what had happened. They were victims of this scheming man, too. You can only imagine how crazy she felt, being cut off from her children's school and not knowing why. Nothing made any sense; nothing added up correctly. This was merely another part of his plan to isolate, humiliate, belittle, and cut her off. Stuck in a box in the corner, she mentally deteriorated. Her ability to function in daily life was shaky because of what this Red Flag Man did in front of her and behind her back. Watching your own back is just one of the many necessary precautions with a Red Flag Man.

When things just don't make sense in your relationship, that situation is not normal and is a warning sign. If you can't see it for yourself, at least consider listening to a loved one or friend trying to point it out for you. Gain all the knowledge you can, and then use your brain wisely instead of letting it get messed up by a Red Flag Man.

You will feel overpowered, controlled, and shocked. Trying to understand how women sit and take such abuse as their minds are attacked led me to this thought: *The shock effect stuns us and renders us immobile.* The things they say and do are so far from what we expect that we just can't believe what we are hearing. We have a scrawny adopted black cat, who once begged at our door, whom my children fed him turkey and ham left over from Thanksgiving. For years now, he has been king of the house and a part of our family. Not realizing his size, he exhibits no fear in defending his home and property line. A neighbor called me one day and said, "Your cat is psychotic!" The story unfolded that Moochie had jumped up on a huge Lab, who walked on our sidewalk. He repeated the action when a friend of mine stopped by to say hello while walking with her big dog. He hissed at the dog and literally kept him from our front porch. The dog was in shock that a little, skinny cat hissed at him and boldly came at him. Both these dogs could have eaten him in one bite, but they stopped and left.

Shock can dumfound us so no words come out. We feel as if we are in the twilight zone. You think, *Is this real? Did he just say that to me?* A pattern easily evolves, and the mental invasion continues. The line has been crossed and will continue to be unless challenged. One woman was speechless when her husband announced, "I am a fine race horse, and your good fortune is to be able to feed and care for me and send me off to the races every day." He was so serious she dared not laugh or stand up for herself. This set the tone for the treatment she endured with this Red Flag Man. Hopefully being conscious of such mental abuse will lessen the shock effect and increase your awareness of what to watch and listen for.

If you cannot see the truth of such a situation, at least consider listening to someone who does see this mind-raping travesty. Knowledge can also help you clean the cobwebs from your mind and see more clearly what is happening to you. But just like the rainbow unnoticed in the sky, you will not see anything if you aren't looking. You may be so downtrodden you cannot realize what is happening. Your mother may have an idea. She may have had the same thing happen to her. At least give her a chance to help. Her vision may be better than yours.

Being with a Red Flag Man over time is like being barely able to see, and what you do see is baffling and muddled at best. Images gradually become blurry, gray areas appear, and your self-doubt creeps in. I hear advertisements on the radio every day that announce, "Blurry vision fixed immediately with Lasik. Wake up and see clearly." I wish it were that simple to fix the hazy vision caused by the Red Flag Man.

Ralph Waldo Emerson said, "People only see what they are prepared to see." I have seen intelligent women caught up in the Red Flag Man's web of disguise and deceit, who are totally ignorant of what is happening mentally to them because they lack knowledge and experience. Knowledge can help you to wake up, see clearly, and think sensibly. The voice of experience from someone who loves and cares about you can confirm your own worries about a Red Flag Man. Then you will be better prepared to assess how you are affected mentally when you are with the Red Flag Man.

You can feel as if you are in a fog and your mind is fuzzy. Years ago I experienced harrowing, foggy driving conditions as I hurried to catch an early flight at JFK airport. I crept along the unfamiliar highway, barely able to see my own windshield. We have to do the same in life sometimes, placing trust in just continuing on the right road. You can end up on the wrong road going nowhere fast if you tolerate mental harassment from a Red Flag Man.

Though your experiences may be frightening and overwhelming, you can make it back to mental stability and good mental health. Blurred vision can lead you to unclear thinking. If you find yourself closing your eyes and shaking your head in frustration and questioning your own sanity, you need help. With appropriate support, that fog will lift, bringing the glorious dawn of a new life of freedom for you. New, clearer, and better days are ahead, with you in charge of your destiny.

One beautiful fall, I visited my son at his boarding school in Blairstown, New Jersey, before the days of navigation systems and online maps. Thankfully, my younger son went with me, or I might still be lost. Late one night we attempted to return to our inn after a program at the school. In that part of the country, it was pitch-black with no streetlights, curbs, or lane markers. Rain made visibility even worse. I had no sense of direction and felt turned around, lost, and scared.

My young son, who to this day is a man of few words, managed to say a few that dark, scary night and calmed me so that I could think clearly enough eventually to find our way to the inn. Being with a Red Flag Man, you will experience some of the same feelings. The happiness that you desire and deserve will not be found under the influence of such ill-treatment. You will feel lost, confused, troubled, and unsure of yourself, and at times, you will feel very scared. With a Red Flag man, you are on a road leading nowhere with your mind getting more muffled by the minute.

Certain behaviors cause mental abandonment. There will be good and bad times, ups and downs, but there will be no hope for improvement and no grounds for rationalizations at all. On my maternal grandparents' ranch, the grandchildren would ride in the back of my Pop Paw's green pick-up truck up and down winding, bumpy dirt roads. We especially loved one hill and had him go up and down because of the roller-coaster effect. I never tired of riding in that truck, even though the dust was prolific and made big clouds behind us.

With a Red Flag Man, the bumps in that road will be terrible setbacks and patterns of behavior that will make you feel mentally lost, abandoned, and alone. The billowing dust will cloud your vision, and you will not even be able to see what is happening to you or understand it. Because mental torment happens slowly and gradually with intermittent hopeful times, you make allowances and excuses. But in the end, the road leads nowhere, leaving only pain, sorrow, and disappointment for you and your future children. The aftermath will require years of recovery to regain all you lost and to restore your mental composure.

Why would you want to get on such a dusty, dead-end road with known roadblocks? In high school, "The Long and Winding Road" was a very popular song. The song speaks of the road leading back to his girlfriend's door. In the context of Red Flag Men, your long and winding road can lead back to your sanity, peace, freedom, and joy. You can avoid the wrong, dangerous roads by noting red flags at the very beginning.

Despite obvious roadblocks, we women often ignore the huge red flags and go around the roadblocks, hoping for the best and falsely thinking our situation will be different. Poor choices will eventually take you nowhere, slowly, painfully, and surely. Hopefully, if you are more aware and armed with knowledge, you can find your way down the right road with a clear head. Don't be another uncounted statistic of mind raping.

Excessive control affects you on a mental level. Are you constantly being put down? Does everything end up being your fault? Are you continually feeling humiliated by this Red Flag Man? Does he refuse to communicate, suffer from extreme moodiness, or withdraw obvious affection from you? Do the words "I love you" seem empty when he says them? Are you broken down to the point of nothingness? Do you feel anxious, scared, or cornered? Do you find yourself crying, apologizing, agonizing, and generally dismayed and unhappy? Do you walk on eggshells? Are you never able to please him? Has his personal power taken over your personal mental state?

Do you feel unusually worried, sad, or stressed most of the time? Have you lost your enthusiasm for life? Are you told what to think? Do you feel intimidated or overpowered? Does your mind feel foggy? Does he go behind your back and do hurtful things? Does what he says shock you? Are you unsure of yourself and your abilities around this

Red Flag Man? Does he exert excessive control over you?

Neglecting yourself can lead to a mental breakdown. Seriously consider these and other pertinent questions concerning how you are affected mentally when you are with a Red Flag Man. Good personal mental health comes from being around positive, uplifting, sincere people. How you feel mentally matters very much and will affect your quality of life. How do you feel mentally when you are with him? Negative mental feelings can easily progress to affecting you physically.

How Are You Affected Physically?

Stress is like an iceberg. We can see one-eighth of it above, but what about what's below?

Unknown

Anyone in the workplace knows getting docked for even one day's pay can potentially mess up a monthly budget. Having sick children causes such problems for many parents at my school; however, sending these sick children with high fever to school is not the answer. Once, a severe viral illness spread down an entire row of my students, causing even more families to get sick and miss school or work. The unfortunate students on that particular row had direct physical consequences by being in close contact with a sick student. It took over two weeks for my class to get back to normal.

Blatantly exposing innocent people to diseases should not be taken lightly, nor should exposure to physical feelings evoked when with a Red Flag Man. Ramifications of various physical symptoms when you are with a Red Flag Man reverberate negatively upon your life exactly like that rampantly spreading virus.

One summer, while carrying supplies to her friend's houseboat, a young girl stumbled right off the pier into the lake. Her hands were so full she couldn't see where the pier ended. She felt shocked as she hit the cool water. The physical consequences included getting soaking wet and twisting her ankle. Some situations that cause physical consequences can be helped or prevented by our making wiser choices. She could have simply watched where she was going.

After acquiring some delightful mini bundt cake pans, my neighbor decided to use them right away. The first time she used them, she filled them too full, so the dough spilled all over the oven, resulting in a huge mess, but the mini cakes tasted great. The second time, she filled them less full, but she still had a mess to clean up. She could have thought to put a cookie sheet under the mini pans to catch the spillover.

She went for a third try. She decided that using a different recipe and adjusting the dough amount in the pans would bring perfect results. This time the cake batter not only spilled over but also caught fire in the oven and filled the kitchen with smoke. Though the cakes were salvaged, she spent hours cleaning the oven yet again.

Those pans were risky, and she should have stayed in the kitchen while baking and been more careful. Her entire house could have burned down because of some mini bundt cakes and her negligence. Her choices could have had serious physical consequences. The same caution applies to a Red Flag Man. Circumstances surrounding your relationship may change, but giving him continual chances remains risky business. You not only jeopardize being affected emotionally and mentally but now physically as well. Initially, you may feel physically sick. Abusive relationships are unhealthy.

One young woman suffered unexplainable stomach cramps and pain. She felt as if she had a continual stomachache and never felt hungry. When she did eat, she often felt worse. Many doctors' appointments revealed nothing. After her wedding, the groom became unusually solemn and indifferent. She internalized her worries and fears, causing her to feel anxious and nervous. Confrontation only made him defensive. She began to doubt herself, feeling as if she just wasn't good enough. Though they had dated for a long time, she discovered that she really didn't know him at all.

In reality, years of unrealized emotional and mental trauma finally caught up with her physically. He would corner her in the small kitchen of their apartment. He laid down the law about the way things were going to be. His total control made her feel trapped, fearful, and confused. She considered leaving, but she worried about where she would go and what she would do. She lacked the strength and self-confidence to break away from the escalating stressful situation. Her stomach pains led to further loss of appetite, depression, and years of other needless physical consequences. She had missed the signs because she lacked knowledge of her rights as a human being in a relationship.

Concerns in the marriage continued to eat away at her, causing physical symptoms with no known medical cause. Many years would pass before she would finally see and understand what was disturbing her—a Red Flag Man.

Another young bride developed Temporomandibular Joint Disorder (TMJ), a problem related to the jaw joint, and began seriously grinding her teeth at night early in her marriage. She went to the dentist and got a mouth guard to sleep in and some tension relief medicine. Every morning her jaw remained dreadfully sore. Even opening her mouth to eat or talk hurt. None of the remedies helped. The abusive oppression of her domineering husband finally resulted in physical symptoms that progressively got worse. Her husband's highs and lows were unpredictable. He broke promises to her. He pushed her to do things she felt uneasy about, leading to muscular tension and pain, asthma symptoms, and weight loss. Physically, she felt like a disaster.

Two weeks into her marriage, another young woman strongly sensed trouble and left, but she unwisely returned upon discovering she was pregnant. Her suffering began with simple things, such as being humiliated and embarrassed in front of her parents and family, an action that Red Flag Men often take in an attempt to isolate and sever family ties. She left again, feeling great stress and fear, and she had her baby while living nearby with her parents.

He turned on the charm and courted her yet again. He stressed that the baby deserved a father, causing her further emotional stress and mental anguish. She felt tense, distraught, and confused, and yet she foolishly relented to his incessant pleadings and gave him yet another chance. Consequential stomach ulcers were just the tip of the iceberg of her physical ailments. They now lived far away from the safety net her parents had provided. She remained trapped with a Red Flag Man.

Unfortunately, her personal, inner physical symptoms were only the beginning of her pain. In her situation, the abuse escalated to outer physical trauma. She still has nightmares of some of the things he did to her. Her life with this Red Flag Man left her emotionally, mentally, and physically terrified.

Denial of any problem works for just so long.

Think of the universal recycling symbol displayed all over the world. Revolving arrows point at each other to indicate a circle that keeps going around continuously. A similar cycle happens with emotional, mental, and physical feelings. They just keep going around in a loop, causing pain and trouble from head to toe as the resultant stress and tensions mount and multiply. Physical problems women endure as a result of that stress are headaches, TMJ, muscle pain, stomach and intestinal problems, decreased fertility, skin problems, weak immune systems, asthma, and chronic pulmonary disease.

The predictable progression of feelings with a Red Flag Man goes from emotional, mental, and finally to physical causing immense stress.

Denial of any problem works for just so long. Effects experienced up to this point have been possibly disguised, suppressed, or rationalized away, either consciously or subconsciously. When physical symptoms arise, denial becomes more difficult, the problems more serious, and issues more complicated. Before, you just felt sad and crazy. Now your body rebels by reacting to all those buried feelings and suffers the consequences in immeasurable, undeniable ways.

When you have been hit in the gut, perhaps your gut feelings will wake up. Your gut feeling or instinctive reaction to something is generally an individual's common-sense perception of what is morally right, and it is valuable and required, especially when dealing with a Red Flag Man. Consider how you can respond to such stressful situations when you are with a Red Flag Man. Response is something you can choose. Your own instincts can guide your responses and choices. Why do women who seem so savvy ignore obvious, pertinent clues, their personal gut feelings, and advice from friends and loved ones when involved with an identified Red Flag Man? When your mother notices and asks you what is wrong, you need to tell her the truth.

Early one drizzly morning, while entering the on-ramp of a major freeway on my way to work, a car jutted in front of me in a split second. I thought, *Get around that car as soon as possible. It spells trouble.* Changing lanes quickly allowed me to get ahead of him. Unfortunately, I got side-tracked listening to the radio. My gut feeling had told me that car was trouble, and I should have been on alert and watched more closely from my rearview mirror. Because of ongoing construction, the lanes were very tight and exits difficult to identify, especially in the rain. Preparing to exit, that same car cut directly in front of me, and we both almost smashed into the guardrail. I couldn't believe my eyes, but I should have believed my gut feeling.

When your mother asks you what is wrong, tell her the truth.

Physical effects cannot be ignored. As physical symptoms crop up all over your body, there will be no denying the fact that something is wrong. Unfortunately, a doctor cannot fix any of it, although he will try to bandage you with every medicine available. As soon as any unusual, unexplainable physical symptom appears while you are with a Red Flag Man, your body may be sending a message of warning to you.

Chronic stress leads to breakdowns and even death. Stress is caused by three categories of stressors: frustration, conflict, and pressure. All three of these thrive in a Red

Flag Man relationship, creating a pressure cooker of anxiety that wears you down day after day, year after year. With no visible means of escape, you feel the stress grind away at your physical health, resulting in dangerous changes to your circulation, heart, and entire nervous system

Such a scenario, for your health's sake, needs attention. Major causes of chronic stress show up as feeling trapped in unhealthy relationships, living in a difficult relationship, and being unable to express feelings. The most dangerous aspect of stress is that the women suffering from it get used to the treatment and then just passively accept it. Doing so adversely affects their physical health now as well as years later.

The ups and downs in such relationships make it hard to leave. It's hard to leave when you love and care about a Red Flag Man. You may fear being alone or believe your partner may hurt you. Talking to someone you can trust is critical. But one thing you need to remember is that violence is never okay.

Recently, a friend confided to me that she suddenly started having daily panic attacks that made her feel light-headed and gave her trouble breathing and momentarily unable to function. Her recent miscarriage had upset her, but most distressing of all is the Red Flag Man she lives with. Over several years, the physical symptoms have slowly risen, following the predictable pattern of related stress. The medicine prescribed will be only a short-term aid. Perhaps knowledge will help her carefully examine her situation and the real cause of her panic attacks. The attacks and other symptoms will haunt her as long as she tolerates the emotional, mental, and physical mistreatment from her Red Flag Man. She remains oblivious to the dangerous picture unfolding and chooses to continue with the status quo.

A very intelligent stockbroker highly recommended a certain stock, and prospects were looking very good for a new cancer drug. He and his family invested heavily. It really looked like a winner. Unfortunately, he did not rate a tip like Martha Stewart. When the FDA did not approve the drug, the stock fell, and everyone took a loss. Life is a risky business, but some things are obviously doomed like two trains coming at a rapid pace towards each other. A head-on collision is inevitable. One of those evident forces is a Red Flag Man. The crash of feelings you experience with him will explode like a firecracker into a plethora of physical ramifications as you experience detrimental physical changes in your body.

If you play with matches, you will eventually get burned or set the house on fire. We had barely moved into our home when one daughter had votive candles burning in her room. She failed to notice some school papers folded too near the flame. The papers caught on fire, and luckily she saw them. She picked up the flaming paper to take to the bathroom sink, but the flame got bigger. She dropped the burning paper on the carpet and called for me. We smothered it with a towel, but we've had to look at that big, black spot for years now. Red Flag Men-related fires are not so easily extinguished, and yet their image is forever burned and imprinted in your mind. The resultant physical symptoms develop slowly inside and outside your body.

Pursuing a course with a Red Flag Man constitutes playing with fire on a different level. You may think you are a mature adult at the ripe old age of twenty-five, thirty-five, or fifty-five. You may not want to hear advice critical to your life, and yet learning possible physical symptoms could spare unfortunate, unnecessary physical consequences. Do you honestly believe your situation is different or that he'll change someday? Listen to the voice of experience. Listen to your mother or a friend.

When physical symptoms afflict your body with no medical cause, you are playing with a ten alarm fire if you choose to ignore the situation. You might not even realize the cause of your physical problems. You will find yourself in a shaky situation, especially when this particular red flag waves in your face.

Why would a person want to take such chances with so much at stake? The medical consequences of stress are no secret. The lifelong scars remain after the fire has been extinguished. Cardiovascular disease from resultant high blood pressure and arrhythmia is a major consequence of acute stress that negatively affects your extended quality of life. Your physical suffering does internal as well as external damage to your body. Thinking more carefully can prevent such unnecessary fires, as well as other negative consequences.

You may even feel symptoms of Post Traumatic Stress Disorder. PTSD often pertains to soldiers returning home from dangerous war zones and the feelings and physical symptoms they experience weeks, months, years, or a lifetime later. Studying this disorder and comparing physical symptoms women face during and after life with a Red Flag Man reveals shocking analogies. Melissa Stoppler, MD, wrote an article describing PTSD as "a person's response to trauma, developing following any traumatic, catastrophic life experience."

Dr. Stoppler listed war, car/airplane crashes, physical abuse, and rape as examples of causes of PTSD. Mind rape qualifies as well. Carefully consider the emotional, mental, and physical symptoms: flashbacks, detachment or estrangement, nightmares, sleep disturbances, family discord, occupational instability, and impaired functioning. What an implausible list of physical consequences correlating directly to symptoms related to how you are affected physically when you are with a Red Flag Man.

Mixed with the common subsequent divorce rate, these effects contribute to a deadly combination. I thought my friend merely suffered from divorce trauma, but after a horrendous experience with a Red Flag Man, clearly the seriousness of her suffering fits the PTSD scenario perfectly. I recall having to take her on simple errands the first few weeks after her husband left her and her children. She suffered from impaired functioning. She battled sleep problems for years, and when she finally did sleep, horrific nightmares of what her husband did to them plagued her.

Unfortunately, her nightmares continued when she woke up. Dealing with her ex-husband, their children, and finances for over ten years nearly destroyed this vibrant lady. She endured continual trauma with her unhappy, shook-up, displaced children. Her stress levels skyrocketed. She suffered further from loss of appetite, chronic depression, anxiety, a sense of being overwhelmed, and a desire to escape or run away.

That adds up to quite a punishment for ignoring red flags while dating and being married to a Red Flag Man. How physical do these symptoms have to be to grab your attention? You will not be immune to the physical symptoms of anxiety, irritability, and depression. Be alert. Be aware. Be smart.

Having a relationship with a Red Flag Man is risky. Nothing will turn out as you expect. You will feel as if you ventured right out into the path of a tornado. No groundwork could be adequate enough to prepare you for the destruction. You have received fair warning. Getting knowledge will benefit you greatly. Ultimately, only you can choose what to do with it.

Some of us remember when the government first required tobacco companies to display the warnings on their products, stating, "Smoking is dangerous to your health." These Red Flag Men need to have warnings attached to them. When you are with them, your health can be in danger. Why would you refuse to leave a level-five hurricane zone despite the evacuation order? Will you heed warnings?

Think vigilantly before flirting with any disaster, especially the Red Flag Man variety because he can be dangerous to your emotional, mental, and especially your physical health. "Everybody sooner or later, sits down to a banquet of consequences," said Robert Louis Stevenson. Choices, and consequences of those choices, matter. Yes, you can make your own choices, but you cannot choose your consequences. Once a poor choice is made, the inevitable sequence of events will unfold despite anything you say or do. This knowledge can help you with that critical decision. Do you see red flags or not?

Rationalization, sympathy, and compassion prove detrimental in such a relationship. When you are attempting to decide on a man in your life, every brain cell in your head needs to be functioning. Red flags are not that hard to see. Red flags do indeed mean something; in fact they are a foreboding, a red foreboding. Dealing with stress long-term in a Red Flag Man relationship can literally wear you out physically.

Before the days of washers and dryers and after the scrub board, people used a contraption called a ringer. You would manually feed wet clothes through it, and when you turned the axle, it would squeeze the water out so the clothes would dry faster. "You put me through the ringer" means something was harrowing, unpleasant, and exhausting, leaving you washed-out, so to speak.

Raising kids definitely puts us through the ringer, as do difficult job assignments, moves, job changes, and other life experiences which temporarily wear us down and challenge us. Such life events are harrowing but mild compared to being put through the Red Flag Man ringer. With him, you will feel exhausted, worn out, left out, and physically out of sorts. If that describes how you may be feeling, your own body is warning you. How you feel being with a Red Flag Man compares to being electrocuted as all your energy is zapped out of you. You don't even realize what you have been through until years later.

How do you describe feeling "totally washed out" emotionally, mentally, and physically? I doubt this could be found in any medical journal. My ninth child was late and weighed almost ten pounds. When a friend asked how I felt after her birth, I replied, "I felt like I'd been run over by a truck." Being physically worn out from the stress of the pregnancy and trying to plan for the eight children at home while I was in the hospital had taken its toll on me. That was nothing compared to what women experience after a Red Flag Man fiasco. You will be washed up, wrung through the ringer, and hung out to dry.

A dear friend recently expressed gratitude for finally, after decades, feeling like herself again and returning back from the dead. Her grown children rejoice at having their mother back. Her life during and after a Red Flag Man left her physically debilitated in numerous ways. She battled anxiety, exhaustion, stomach problems, and jaw trouble in addition to diminished interaction with friends, insomnia, and depression. She did what she had to do to finish raising her children, sacrificing her own welfare all the while. Finally she recovered and can rejoice in life once more after too many wasted, useless, physically damaging and exhausting years.

One woman literally wished she could trade places with a friend battling cancer. This dying woman wanted so desperately to live and finish raising her children, while the other would have gladly given up her life out of desperation, despair, and depression from the aftermath of her tragic life and divorce from a Red Flag Man. She felt she could not bear more of the same for endless years ahead. The overwhelming obstacles and continual harassments involved in the shared raising of her children left her despondent and totally drained. Ultimately, that describes what it feels like physically with a Red Flag Man.

A woman recently told a group of friends how much she missed the human touch, living alone. What is the price for companionship? Those of you having it on a daily basis cannot understand the huge gap its absence leaves in your life. Perhaps some can handle being alone better than others. Some women put up with a lot to avoid that. You need to be comfortable with yourself alone. If you are not, you will be unable to make a good choice in a man. Anything or any man is better than nothing to some women, despite all the negative physical feelings.

Women are affected physically in two categories by a Red Flag Man: inwardly, and less obviously, or outwardly with bruises, burns, fractures, and cuts. If you suffer any such symptoms, they spell danger. Your initial symptoms present as stress, concerning the relationship. Is he extremely jealous or controlling? Is he capable of injuring you? Do you have even an ounce of fear that the Red Flag Man could and would hurt you? Do you feel tense when he is around? Do you have a danger plan?

More inwardly, you might battle TMJ, muscle pain, asthma, anxiety, panic attacks, depression, or stomach problems. Are you always trying to keep the peace and not make him angry? Has he verbally threatened you, saying, "You'll be sorry"? Such issues cannot be taken lightly. Have any of these ailments impaired your sleep or affected your ability to function? At what point for you is the line drawn concerning how you are affected physically when you are with this Red Flag Man? The sooner you make your own discovery about the Red Flag Man, the fewer mistakes you will have to correct.

Could you describe yourself as a "physical wreck"? Is your stress level affecting how you feel and act? These and other real, physical symptoms can be directly related to your relationship with a Red Flag Man and should be of great concern to you. How are you doing physically when you are with him? What are you willing to do about it?

There comes a time when you have to decide what, if anything, to do. You stand at a fork in the road, a time of reckoning. You do not stand there alone. Many women have stood there before you, perhaps even your own mother or a close friend. She may be waiting cautiously yet anxiously to help with your serious decision. You may benefit from her life experiences. You may also regret not hearing about them until too late.

Having learned about all the characteristics of a Red Flag Man and how you are affected emotionally, mentally, and physically when you are with him, you face the question, "What will you do now?" Your own personal peace and happiness depend on how you use the knowledge you have gleaned to take appropriate action. You and possibly future generations could have to pay the price for what you decide.

PART THREE

What Do You Do for Yourself?

I have been impressed with the urgency of doing. Knowing is not enough, we must apply. Being willing is not enough, we must do.

Leonardo da Vinci

chapter fourteen

Be Smart

*Wisdom is knowing what to do next, skill
is knowing how to do it, and virtue is
doing it.*

David Starr Jordan

Scouting for athletic teams appears to be a fun job, although it entails a lot of traveling and watching endless numbers of games and films. When scouts watched one of my daughters play volleyball, they were impressed. As a left-handed outside hitter, she executed kills that were effective and powerful. They did not have to watch long to realize her leadership skills, determination, and resiliency on the court and off as well. They made a smart choice offering her a college scholarship. She played well and maintained a 4.0 grade point average.

Skill, self-confidence, and natural ability show up readily during athletic events. Unfortunately, scouting a Red Flag Man can be more challenging. He looks good in person and on paper. His expertly framed Harvard degree looks impressive above his Wall Street office desk. He could be any woman's dream, appearing dressed impeccably in a special order designer suit. However, his complicated game plan proves harder to decipher, is sometimes devious and frequently misleading. Many things in life don't live up to their packaging.

Another daughter succeeded in a different way of competing. She rigorously trained for a year for an academic competition. The impressive first place medals hanging around her neck made all her hard work worth it. Her academic triathlon team took first place in eighth grade, a glorious occasion for celebration. In real life, you will need more than a high IQ or athletic ability to spot a Red Flag Man and know what to do about him.

Armed with knowledge, you won't be fooled.

Advertising is a huge, calculated business. Consider how much money companies pay to get ten seconds for an ad during the Super Bowl. How many times have we been duped by the calculated sugarcoating of sales and advertising? Recently, studying some car information online caused me to set up an appointment with the dealership and test-drive a particular car. Having looked it over, I went into the dealing room. The paper the salesman set in front of me did not even closely resemble the paper I had printed from the Internet. Upon comparing the drastically different numbers, the salesman quickly had an explanation, but the truth was that the ad was just a ploy.

Such sugarcoated advertising had one goal in mind: to get me there and make a sale. This time I surprised myself. I walked out after saying, "No, thanks anyway!" We need to draw the line more often and beware the fantasy deal. Awareness will help us make smarter choices. Women especially need to watch out for shady dealings with Red Flag Men.

Sugarcoating paints a fairy-tale picture that is in direct opposition to the reality of life. Red Flag Men shine as master sugar coaters extraordinaire, causing many unsuspecting women to fall into their traps. These Red Flag Men inflate their lives with materialism and self-praise which makes them look and seem like the find of the century. Armed with knowledge, you won't be fooled.

You may feel miserable around this type of man, but he will tell you what a prize he is, further confusing you. He will always tell you that you have all the problems and need help. Realize the truth and sensibly deal with it. Be smart, and you will be free to be your wonderful self and live a peaceful, abuse-free life with or without a Red Flag Man.

If it sounds too good to be true, it usually is. At some time, we have all been victims of the luring power of advertising and have succumbed to its enticements. While recently washing my hair with a very special shampoo that I ordered from an ad in a nice woman's magazine, I smiled. I still can't believe my eyes when I look at the petite bottle. The clever ad promised shiny, full hair "like the stars in Hollywood," so I fell for it and ordered. At least I did not succumb to the additional sales gimmick to order two bottles and get free shipping. It cost me $35.00, plus shipping that was $7.95. I couldn't wait for it to arrive in the mail. My first clue was the size of the package when it did arrive. Wrapped inside was a tiny bottle and nothing special. Neglecting to read the fine print, I saw only the "promise and dream of beautiful hair." My hair looked the same, and I had had such high hopes. They were totally unrealistic and unfounded but a common experience for us women.

As a child, I remember watching simple yet luring ads on black-and-white television. They had the same mesmerizing effect on children then as they do now. I literally begged my mom to buy Trix cereal. She occasionally succumbed to our whining. The first time, after fixing myself a big bowl, I proceeded to devour the entire serving and immediately waltz outside. I stood on a high ledge in our front driveway and jumped off, totally expecting to fly just like the children in the ad on television. That wasn't a smart idea.

Shocked, I landed on the ground. We women are not the only suckers out there, but we are suckers when latching on to a man with red flags waving in all directions. You will land a lot harder than I did that day if you don't try to be wise in determining what is beneath all the sugarcoating of a Red Flag Man. Remember, in all situations, be smart and realize you have options.

Yes, we women can be kind, nurturing, and attentive. We may love to take care of a man who appears to need us. Beware ending up trapped in an unhealthy, one-sided relationship. You could possibly be trapped doing all the dirty work, getting ignored, and making excuses for his rudeness, abruptness, and lack of appreciation towards you. The mothering eventually gets old, and you just want him to grow up.

Why do you pathetically accept this lopsided scenario and then take and tolerate abusive treatment? My daughter recently told a married friend the title of my book with a brief synopsis, and the friend jovially replied, "They're all Red Flag Men!" She obviously loves and has learned to live amiably with her Red Flag Man. This option certainly works for some. Finding what works and is tolerable for you is very important.

The mothering eventually gets old, and you just want him to grow up.

Remember the importance of mutual respect as you share work and responsibilities with sincere love and appreciation for each other. Your knowledge can assist you in being smart enough to find healthy, stable situations with a man. Patience will be required on your part.

So many times lives are put on hold, waiting to hear from a job interview, waiting for health test results, waiting for a new baby, waiting for an IRS refund, waiting, waiting, and more waiting. You know the story. How do you make the waiting times in your life tolerable and even productive? That seems to be the million-dollar question. You certainly don't want to stall while waiting for a Red Flag Man to change his ways. You want to be smart.

Life is what happens while we are waiting. We sing a beautiful song in my first-grade class on someone's birthday. The incredible words give me chills every time we sing it, saying, "On the day that you were born, the flowers bloomed and the unicorn danced and sang the whole day long / On the day that you were born." The day of your birth signified a special event. Each of us has within us all we need to succeed and make the most of our precious life. Our responsibility requires being smart and carefully thinking things through.

Everything you need to be happy is contained inside you. A man is not necessary for any of that to happen. Sharing your life with the *right* man will compliment and add to your own special life. If you allow it, a Red Flag Man can stifle, snuff out, and completely destroy all that is in you, making fulfilling your personal potential impossible. Put aside the romance and wipe the stars from your eyes long enough to be realistic and assess your situation. Your man may be absolutely great and wonderful. If you are hesitating in any way for any reason, there may be a problem.

Halt, think, and write about it if that helps you. Take the time to analyze what is really going on and what you need to do. Many women find journaling and writing to be not only therapeutic but also informative. Get out the red marker and underline areas of concern, because underlining selections in red in your journal entries identifies your warnings. Red flags mean "recognize the danger," "stop," and "think."

Red flags appear as important indications that mean you need to be smart for the sake of your future. Everything is at stake. Don't be fooled by flashy ads when your entire life is on the line. Read the fine print and handle things appropriately. Singer and author Pearl Bailey said, "You never find yourself until you face the truth." Be smart enough to recognize the truth about a Red Flag Man, look at your options from all angles, and then make the best decision for you.

Intelligently making decisions concerning the rest of our lives requires more than luck. Even a squirrel can make a smart choice. How many times have you had a frisky squirrel run out in the road in front of your car? You quickly decide whether to slow down, slam on your brakes, swerve to miss hitting the animal, or just keep going and hope for the best. Sometimes the lucky squirrel makes it safely across the street against all odds with cars coming fast in both directions. If you are smart, you will allow yourself adequate time to make big decisions.

You are on the road of life, however, and have critical choices of your own to make. If you choose to have a relationship with or marry a Red Flag Man, you could be taking a risk. Either way you choose to go from there, back to your previous life or on with a Red Flag Man, you are in charge of your own life. Your destiny rests in your own hands.

The consequences remain either way. Generally, you have more than a few critical seconds to decide. You must take note if a Red Flag Man tries to rush you with such a significant decision. That alone can raise red flags. You have a brain as well as supportive friends and family members who care deeply for you. Resist stubborn tendencies and turn to loved ones for help. If you find yourself seeing multiple red flags, decision time confronts you. Be smart, patient, and careful as you make the most important decision of your life.

Be bold enough to make better choices. Women today appear to make wiser choices where men are concerned, and yet the divorce rate in this country remains high. Are we women so driven by our hearts that we refuse to use our brains about men? Use the knowledge at your fingertips to help you, and add the benefits of experience through consulting your mother, close relative, or good friend.

A teacher worried about nearing thirty, desperately wanting to be married and have children. Numerous red flags were flying, trying to alert her. Her Red Flag Man had been in trouble with the law, had difficulty keeping a job, had terrible credit along with other financial issues, and did not always tell her the truth. She married him and had two precious children. Unfortunately, the irresponsible Red Flag Man husband left her after the second child was born, still couldn't keep a job, and got arrested again.

Following their divorce, she does a juggling act as the

only parent and primary breadwinner. She will also be battling and dealing with that Red Flag Man for twenty more years because of her sons. You deserve better odds. There are no guarantees in this life, but smart choices increase your odds.

Collecting child support, arranging visitations, sharing birthdays, and alternating holidays cause continual pain and frustration. The look on her face tells the story. The look of a good, kind woman who got royally messed up by a Red Flag Man does not make a pretty sight. Being smart, she saw the signs, but she took a chance anyway. Is the catastrophe and gamble worth the chance? What kind of legacy and example do we leave our children, the innocent victims of our follies? Can words of warning supersede the poor example of a red-flag father and a divorced home? Did she go against her better, smart judgment?

As the American family disintegrates, who will be raising these children? The single, working parents are too exhausted to do much in the evenings. Television and video games present terrible substitutes for loving time with parents. If we women are not making smart choices, needless suffering will destroy many lives. How many red flags must be waved in front of us? How much heartache must we bear?

You owe it to yourself to be informed and to know all you can before you make any big decision or choice. Exercising caution in making decisions will be helpful in all aspects of your life. Take advantage of good old-fashioned experience. When going back to teaching after being out of the workforce for over thirty years, I found the greatest help was talking to experienced teachers who lovingly and willingly guided and helped me back into the job. Survival would have been impossible without these human hands helping me, no matter how much training or reading I did. Carefully consider getting help from those who have been an example to you: family, extended family, neighbors, religious leaders, therapists, and friends.

Because I Said So, the movie with Diane Keaton, takes this point to an extreme. The mother's constant interfering in her daughters' lives was exaggerated, though it emphasized her genuine, well-meaning love. In this movie, the mother said to one of her daughters, "Don't make a mistake that will ruin your life." You would say that to someone you really care about. Any association with a Red Flag Man has such potential in your own life. Will you carefully consider this advice?

Those who love you have learned some pretty hard life lessons, and you can benefit from their mistakes whenever possible. Keep your ears open for help and advice from those who love you. Being temporarily blinded to Red Flag Man antics may cause you obstinately to ignore their valuable advice. Granted, initial signs appear subtly at first when you are lost in the swept-off-your-feet stage. Another pair of eyes comes in handy at such a time. Your choices create your life.

A radio story recently caught my ear, reporting that one in four teenagers has received at least one demeaning, threatening, or abusive text message. What terrible news. Verbal and emotional abuse slips into our children's lives at an early age before they are adequately prepared. We need to inform them of their rights to be abuse-free in every way. They live in tenuous situations, trying to be popular and get invited to parties, but we have to let them know that being abused isn't the way. Teaching by example will help our daughters to stand up for themselves and know where to draw the line. You need to be vigilant.

Consider how even children can exemplify the quality of being observant that will ultimately help them make smarter choices. After having an ingrown toenail cut out, I discovered that neglecting it had caused a fungus to spread, causing more trouble and treatments for months. Because it was at the beginning of sandal season, I bought designer Band-Aids to wear to cover up my infected toe. One day, two separate students noticed and said, "Ms. Bertrand, we can tell your mood by the Band-Aid that you wear." I had a bad cold that day and had worn a plain Band-Aid instead of Strawberry Shortcake, Care Bears, or Curious George. They had noticed my fling for fashion on my big toe. Noticing details is a good skill to develop. Looking, listening carefully, and paying attention to important details in a *man* will especially be to your advantage. If first graders can notice trivial things like my toe, you as an adult can notice significant things about Red Flag Men.

To see and observe, you must consciously be looking. One March, I literally brought spring right into my classroom in the form of an incredible weeping willow miniature tree in four stages of blooming. The first day, there were only tiny buds and a few catkins, or fuzzy blossoms. Before the end of that day, a few tiny, green leaves had appeared. The next day those leaves had grown larger, plus more had appeared. My students had a wonderful time making observations and watching the progress of spring through my guided instruction. You will miss very important things in life if you neglect looking and watching for them.

Verbal and mental questions will come more readily if you are in a smart observation mode. Some of those Red Flag Man concerns might just pass you by or take you over before you realize what is happening. Important details which warrant noticing about this Red Flag Man stand out for us women. Being observant, you will notice potential problems sooner and will proceed with more caution. You will ask more questions out loud and silently ponder others inside your mind.

One of my daughters heard a great story on the radio driving home one weekend which illustrates this point perfectly. In a humorous way, this story illustrates how family traditions begin for various, even ridiculous reasons. Being observant is smart. At holiday time, a new bride was cooking her first ham. She followed the tradition of her mother and cut one end of the ham off before putting it in the oven to bake. This confused her husband who asked why on earth she did that, and she answered, "Because that's the way my mother always did it." He suggested that they call her mother to find out why. Her mother said that she did it just because her mother had always done it. When they called the grandmother, she said, "I don't know why you cut off one end of the ham, but I did it because my pan was too small."

Over the years, she had simply not bought a larger pan and had inadvertently perpetuated a needless tradition for several generations without even knowing it. The same thing can happen to us if we are oblivious and not careful with our decisions. Generations can literally be affected for good or ill.

Today is a good day to start. You can make a good beginning that will lead to a favorable ending and start the positive cycle all over again. Make a point to be smart and watch for the specific red flags you have been made aware of in this book. Make a mental note and then record it in your journal. Be smart by not being fooled and taking the time to find out what works for you. Be realistic and recognize the truth when you see it. Be bold and heed the obvious red flags. Intelligently apply the knowledge you have acquired. Get your facts straight by being observant and asking questions.

A Yiddish Proverb says, "If you don't want to do something, one excuse is as good as another." It's just that those excuses will catch up with you eventually, and it won't be a pretty sight. Your personal efforts to investigate a Red Flag Man will be well worth your efforts. Be smart.

chapter fifteen

Be Sure of Yourself

Build today, then, strong and sure,
With a firm and ample base;
And ascending and secure
Shall tomorrow find its place.

Henry Wadsworth Longfellow

A college student changed his major more than the usual two or three times before getting his degree. He still didn't really know what he wanted to do when and if he ever grew up. He was anything but sure of himself and certainly not in any state of mind to be a lifelong partner. Countless such situations exist where couples have comfortably "gone together" for many years with no engagement in sight, but the woman keeps waiting and hoping for a ring and ceremony while continuously extending how much longer she will wait. Will such a Red Flag Man ever grow up and be ready? If these women were surer of themselves, would they waste the best years of their lives in such a manner? How many chances and years does a Red Flag Man need and deserve to figure out what he really wants?

One summer, my father bought a new blue and white station wagon, and then he announced that we were driving to Disneyland in California. My mother had only a few days' notice to arrange for our pets, mail, and plants, and then pack up our family of six. She expertly did so and had us ready to leave very early one morning. Dad knew the exact route we would take, had arranged motels along the way, and had contacted our cousins in California. He showed utmost confidence in where we were going and how we would get there.

Knowing who you are before going full steam into a relationship would be equally advisable. Having confidence and trust in yourself first creates a strong, safe base necessary for when you do have a healthy relationship with a man. Being secure and satisfied with yourself helps you know where you are headed and with whom you might like to share your life. Discovering and then solidifying who you are initially serves to help you know where to draw the line about what is acceptable and tolerable for you in how you desire to be treated. Then you can better judge how long to wait and if the man is worth waiting for.

Ayn Rand, a Russian-born United States novelist, said, "Learn to value yourself, which means to fight for your happiness." We aren't necessarily born with self-confidence, and no one has it all the time. As women, who often instinctively focus on everyone but ourselves, developing that critical self-assurance often gets ignored and then forgotten. Even after we develop a healthy self-confidence level, it can be extinguished as slowly and silently as it appeared, especially with a Red Flag Man.

Thankfully, rebuilding strength in yourself throughout your lifetime, at any age, can happen. The main ingredient is your strong desire to do so.

Years ago, I went to a new friend's home for brunch. I had high expectations as she was rumored to be an excellent cook, but the conversation proved more interesting than the omelets. She unintentionally revealed what she had given up of herself in sacrifices for her marriage. While discussing her interesting dishes, she noted she had display plates to match, but her husband insisted the walls be plain and unadorned. She mentioned foods she loved but no longer served because he didn't like them. She enjoyed conversation, but he insisted on silence in the mornings. She didn't agree with his treatment of their children, but he had the last say in the discipline.

On my way home, I calculated all her words in my mind, like money into a cash register, and realized her life did not present a very pretty picture. I felt sorrow that two such great people had gotten stuck in such a terrible rut that eventually led to divorce. Their life together could have been different.

Though she was married to a definite Red Flag Man, if she had believed and trusted more in herself and her intrinsic worth, perhaps they could have effectively compromised and built an equalized, satisfactory, rewarding marriage together. Since the divorce, she has come alive, decorating her house according to her own cheerful taste, and has enjoyed doing all the things she had deprived herself of during her marriage. With understanding, communication, compromise, and commitment, this couple could have made those things happen within the marriage setting had she been surer of herself at the onset.

By becoming a self-empowered woman, you can make your efforts to get what you deserve in a relationship to pay off. Sometimes our own ignorance keeps us from knowing for sure what that entails. Scott Peck aptly reminds us of what you need and deserve from love and relationships in his book, *The Love You Deserve*. Every person on this planet desires to be loved and cherished. You deserve unity, kindness, honesty, your own dreams, equality, intimacy, love for yourself, and pure spirituality.

Peck's chapter on self-empowered womanhood reminds us that we are first-class citizens. He challenges women to have a "clear sense of their empowered role" thus elevating the status of womanhood to an acceptable equality with men. What will it take for you to cherish yourself enough not to settle for second-best? This goes along with warnings of danger to women who say, "He's the best I've found." They even say, "He has most of the qualities I am looking for, and I am thirty." A better idea is to think, *I am not willing to compromise all that I am by settling for less than I deserve.* Do not allow self-doubts to paralyze you or cause you to make poor choices.

You not only deserve better, but you also must demand it. Don't give up your freedom, dignity, and potential destiny for the comfort of momentary security by allowing a Red Flag Man to drain your life rather than enhance it. With this empowerment comes much responsibility, and your first responsibility remains to yourself to make wise choices concerning everything in your life, especially choosing a man. Somewhere between your glorious birth and twenty-first birthday, that innate love for yourself somehow gets dissolved, muffled, or mixed-up. In fact, it can get confused for women at any age.

An empowered woman will take charge of her own life, knowing where to draw the line, which will help her recognize when to stay and when to go. Loving yourself frees you to reach your potential and be independent. Your peace of mind and your quality of life hang in the balance. In the end, your critical choices will determine your life.

A great inner wisdom as your own personal resource exists in your very soul, just waiting to be tapped into and used. You may have to get away temporarily from the situation. It's the proverbial can't-see-the-forest-for-the-trees adage. Get away and find a quiet place where you can get in touch with your inner self. Reread your journal. Ponder what you have written. Think objectively about what you are experiencing. If you are struggling, realize the need to talk to your mother or other interested friend or relative. Reflect upon crucial things you deserve such as love, respect, kindness, joy, and an abuse-free life. Sometimes the truth of the matter becomes crystal clear as your reread you journal. Will you listen to your messages to yourself?

Will you listen to those who love you?

Every dawn presents you with a new day to get what you deserve from life. You choose the path to receive all that you deserve with or without a man. You will be empowered, and nothing will be able to stop or deter you. You can have a new life on your own. What is right will find its way to you. You will be able to enjoy the moment in all of its splendor and glory. Begin today with a thought that grows into an action, and then with one baby step at a time move forward until you feel this intangible empowerment for yourself.

I remember taking a family trip to visit relatives in San Antonio before I started pre-school. My mother used the occasion to have my "blankie" disappear while we were there. Some college students take a special stuffed animal from their childhood with them. Sometimes primary-age students suck their thumbs when they get tired in the afternoons. We have all seen large toddlers with pacifiers in their mouths and wanted to take the pacifiers away. Depending on the circumstances, we temporarily satisfy our neediness. Such dependence marks the antithesis of the strength and independence that we need to have in becoming self-empowered women so we can take control of the decisions that impact our lives.

Dr. Wayne Dyer speaks of this in his wonderful book, *Ten Secrets for Success and Inner Peace.* The first chapter is dedicated to the principle of having your mind "open to everything and attached to nothing." Dr. Dyer teaches that if you let go of your "attachments" or the sources of all your problems, then your mind can be open to limitless potential. Being self-empowered puts you more in control of your life, leaving you less tempted to make wrong choices with a Red Flag Man or allow yourself to be run over by him, his choices, and his desires. Sometimes just speaking up rationally and discussing things logically begins the compromising process and makes a good life together possible.

Dr. Dyer advises, "Never let your happiness or success depend on an attachment to any thing, any place, and particularly, any person." If you find the right person to spend your life with, you will be able to love him for exactly who he is, and you will be able to be yourself. Suze Orman is another amazing speaker and author who embodies this self-empowerment on a different level. As a financial expert, she speaks to women of being smart in managing their finances and "having the power to turn things around." She reminds us how we need to meet our potential and save ourselves. We women can be natural nurturers and caregivers, but Suze says to "be generous with yourself" and don't be afraid to say when you need something. Being sure of yourself will benefit you in all aspects of your life, especially when dealing with a Red Flag Man.

First imagine how good things can be for you. Recognize that this self-empowerment can assist you in knowing when to say "no" to an unhealthy relationship or abuse of any kind. There are most definitely red flags in financial situations, job-related situations, and relationships. As a self-empowered woman, take note of any and all red flags in your path and then have the courage to take the appropriate, necessary actions. If you trust yourself with the power that is within you, life can be good, and you can make good things happen.

You obviously cannot control the weather or what others choose to do, but you can control yourself. You will not be given the perfect circumstances, but you can work to bring about your full potential and personal happiness. Your life rests in your control. I recall when a group of girls planned and prepared for months for a summer camping experience. They had been diligent through months of preparation to ensure a successful week of camping. Expert adult campers took off work to take the girls and teach them for the week. After extensive packing, they were on their way to a lovely campsite by a lake several hours away from their homes. They got there safely and took hours setting up their tents, cooking supplies, and sleeping bags overlooking the lake. The one thing they couldn't be sure of turned out to be the weather.

Late that evening, the phone rang with news of a terrible storm that had come upon their campsite. The park officials had ordered the sight to be vacated because of possible flooding. In a downpour, they threw everything back into the vans and trucks and took off towards home. They appeared several hours later drenched, exhausted, and very disappointed as the leaders delivered the girls to their homes in the wee hours of the morning.

Assume responsibility by controlling what you can.

I got a call the next day to come retrieve their supplies that had been dumped in a leader's backyard. I have never seen such a mess. We gathered what we recognized and never saw some of the things we packed. The simple lesson rang clear: some things like acts of nature are totally out of our control. Despite expert preparations, the weather simply overruled them. Many situations in life are out of our control, but many are in our control if we step up to the plate and assume that responsibility. Be sure by controlling what you can. That is something positive you can do.

Beloved author and illustrator of children's books, Dr. Seuss, said, "Today is your day! Your mountain is waiting, so . . . get on your way." We can be self-empowered women. Focus on the things that you can control by recognizing the options available to you. Seriously consider your choices and the incredible power you have to make wise ones. Then you will discover that self-empowerment that has been within you all along. You can do it.

When my children were in their early years of elementary school, they often got invited to play at one of their friends' houses after school. I practiced extreme caution in this area in order to be sure my children were safe wherever they went. First, we had the child over to monitor how he or she interacted with my child and to get to know the parents personally. I asked critical questions such as checking to see if they had a pool, dogs, teenagers, and supervision.

I learned the hard way that some parents' idea of having a child over to play involved sending them unsupervised to the school playground down the street for hours. In our world today, that just isn't safe or acceptable anymore. Checking first can spare you tragic consequences, especially when Red Flag Men are concerned.

Joyce L. Vedral, author of *Get Rid of Him*, embodies the spirit of the self-empowered woman. In her book, she says, "You know how to get a man, keep a man, and please a man." Her book is how to get rid of a man that is bad for you who is "stealing your time, your energy, and, in effect, your life." Take these thoughts a step backwards. Perhaps we are failing sufficiently to screen these men before we even go on a date.

Being aware of red flags waving so obviously all around these Red Flag Men, before the fact, will spare you unnecessary problems. You will be spared having to get rid of him and will know everything before it seems too late. You owe such due diligence to yourself at least to look around you and learn from what you see so you can be sure. Perhaps you do not know how to pick a man after all. Heavy, serious consequences could weigh you and your future children down with one life-altering choice.

John F. Kennedy Jr. made a tragic, life-altering choice. This young, confident, though inexperienced, pilot chose to fly his new airplane when he wasn't fully trained. Authorities surmise the ensuing darkness distorted his perception, causing him not to be able to properly fly his plane. He, his wife, and his sister-in-law flew straight down to the bottom of the ocean floor. Confidence must be tempered with wisdom.

One of my teenage daughters seemed very sure of herself, believing that she was ready to drive on her own, but she was headed down a road of unwise choices. She had attended driver's education classes and had practiced driving, but she had an agenda of her own. Against my better judgment, she got a brand new car. My warnings about her not being ready to drive at night went unheeded.

One afternoon she went to a friend's house and got preoccupied until darkness set in. She headed home anyway. A block from home, she misjudged a left-hand turn and was hit broadside and spun around. Her new car ended up being totaled before the title even arrived in the mail. Luckily, she was perfectly safe without a scratch. Misjudgments don't always turn out so favorably, especially with Red Flag Men.

You too will find your life crashing down in front of you if you neglect these red flags and choose to ignore them. They will continue to wave and warn whether you take note or not. Why would you choose to ignore warnings? People ignore hurricane warnings and refuse to leave an evacuation area. I always just shake my head when I see those stories. People can be stubborn and too optimistic in the face of danger. How much better to be self-empowered and build healthy relationships, not red-flag ones.

You want to make wise choices and have a happy life. You just have to minimize the pull of your heart and maximize the use of your brain. You were born with a caring, nurturing, loving, comforting, huge heart which serves you well in compassion towards others. But that same heart can also signal your downfall when it comes to choosing a man. You can live fully and passionately and still use your brain. You cannot be sure if you use your heart alone.

Hearts tend to ignore warnings and push red flags aside. Hearts rationalize and overlook critical facts. Hearts set us up to get broken, crushed, demolished, and scarred for the rest of our lives. No matter what your age, your brain must be put to the task for which it was intended, to make wise choices, to see those red flags, and heed their warning. Your mother or someone you are close to could be an integral part of assisting you with such a huge task.

Appreciate yourself. Be sure of yourself. Focus on all that is good. Seek out new and better possibilities as you feel the strength and power that comes from being a self-empowered woman today. In the United States, we believe that we live in the greatest country in the world, where opportunities abound for us as women. Many prominent women are setting an example every day. Recently the majority in the congress switched parties. The president is no longer dealing with a majority of his own party, and for the first time a woman is speaker of the house. As single women, we just took over the United States in a recent census. Over fifty percent of women in our country are living singly, and we are not alone. This brings the United States into uncharted territory, which ironically is how it was founded.

We are on the forefront of a new state of the union. Be glad and thankful for your state, single or married. You have immeasurable potential in either situation. Your future shines brightly, and hope abounds. Self-empowered women need to arise, rejoice, thrive, and support each other.

Denis Waitley, author and motivational speaker, said, "There are two primary choices in life: to accept conditions as they exist or to accept the responsibility for changing them." Please know how very much you matter. You are special. Love and appreciate yourself. Be true to yourself. Everything you do, think, and dream matters. Believe that your life is important to you and to the world. You deserve happiness. You have a good head on your shoulders, and you need to use it. Rudyard Kipling said, "If you can keep your head when all about you / Are losing theirs and blaming it on you / Yours is the Earth and everything that's in it."

You have talents. Use them or lose them. Extend yourself. Do what you love. Pursuing your own interests naturally lifts your spirits. You have a right to enjoy a peaceful life. You are stronger than you think, so trust your inner instincts. When you feel something isn't right, you need to trust yourself. Explore all your options. Just hang in there and be patient. Life is difficult but possible. Poet Emily Dickinson wrote, "For each ecstatic instant / We must an anguish pay / In keen and quivering ratio / To the ecstasy."

Consider this remarkable story about a woman who was true to herself despite losing everything. Many women who marry Red Flag Men choose to stay despite abuse of all kinds for the sake of their children. They usually don't have the finances to hire high-powered attorneys, nor can they afford to care for their children on their own. My friend put up with her husband for years. He never could keep a job or provide consistently for their large family. She even got into the Mary Kay cosmetic business and earned a new car by working long and hard. Looking back, she probably stayed because she knew how powerful his parents were, and she did not want to lose her children. Her life ended up totally different from what she expected when she mistakenly married a Red Flag Man.

When divorce finally happened, his parents came up with money for him to hire an attorney. She was booted out to a tiny apartment where she could barely pay her bills. She got very minimal visitation with the children she dearly loved, had mothered, and raised for years. He later had a heart attack and died. She still did not get cus-tody of the children. His well-to-do parents got custody and moved them to another state. She has suffered all this with grace, poise, and dignity. Being sure of herself has enabled her to begin a new life on her own. You hear a few horror stories like that, and you sit tight in that situation for one reason only, a mother's love and devotion. But should you? What do you do? Can you be sure?

One Red Flag Man planned his divorce a year in advance. He hid money in offshore accounts and carefully calculated every detail of the upcoming separation. His clueless wife came home one day to find her things packed and divorce papers on the table with no warning, no explanation, and no hope of reconciliation. He even had the paperwork in motion to get full custody of their children. In a day, she lost her husband, children, home, financial security, and, in fact, her whole life. Her Red Flag Man had no problem carrying out his business as usual, but luckily she valued herself and slowly recovered and started over, gratefully free of that Red Flag Man.

You can live a productive, happy, single life if you don't get lucky enough to meet one of those good, honest, trustworthy, respectable, kind, and real men. Be true to yourself and get on with the rest of your wonderful life.

For years a friend unintentionally tortured herself putting up the old family Christmas tree. The boxes of old ornaments were filled with memories of her past life, and every Christmas, just touching them saddened her and brought back the pain, the questions, and the intense loss of a whole family. Holidays were difficult for her, as they are for most women and their children in broken home situations because of their initial poor choices in men.

Finally the time came when we she took a brave step forward. For her, taking action meant much more than out with the old and in with the new. She could get a tree she wanted and decorate it with pink ornaments and balls just as she liked which proved to be a silent but strong statement. Every time she walked by the new tree, she smiled and wondered why on earth she had waited so many long, grueling years. The answer to that is parental sacrifice. Women sacrifice to try to maintain some stability in their torn lives, especially for their children, but they shouldn't forget themselves in the process.

You can choose your path, but you cannot choose the consequences. Freedom to make your own choices remains an important principle. In this great country, you have been given the freedom to choose along with the knowledge to choose wisely. Please listen to those who love you. Daughters listen to your mothers. They desire to spare you from making similar mistakes. After listening to them, make your own choice, remembering that future generations could be affected. Your choices are yours, but the consequences are too.

One grandmother silently and painfully continued to suffer for forty years after her initial mistake of marrying a Red Flag Man. She had no idea of the endless ramifications that would hurt everyone involved for decades. She could not have foreseen the divorce or the resultant pain for her, her children, and even the grandchildren at every special occasion and holiday. You have no excuse for not knowing. You can make wiser choices, not only for yourself but also for your posterity.

Take notes whenever you see a positive family situation. Doing so can help you be more sure of yourself and what you want in a good, healthy relationship. A recent visit with one daughter who had a new baby opened my eyes to how couples can and should respectfully interact. They have jobs, work together at home, and love and care for their infant daughter. He gets what they need from the store, changes the baby in the middle of the night, and gives her to my daughter to feed. He gathers trash from the house and takes it out. He helped with decorations for Christmas, exhibiting cooperation and mutual respect. Red Flag Men have a problem with that.

A mother, ill herself, struggled to care for all of her children who had the flu. Can you imagine having a high fever and having to care for many ill children? She would get up and make the rounds, giving them all Tylenol and putting movies on for them, and then collapse into bed until the next one cried out. When she asked her Red Flag Man husband if he could stay home and help, she was told to hire someone. Women deserve so much more than that. Hope exists for you if you stop and carefully consider your dealings with a Red Flag Man and how being with him can affect your quality of life.

A very popular talk show host in Dallas shared her life story on the radio over eight years. She seemed successful, bright, and sure of herself. Coming from a divorced home, she wanted a stable relationship and family more than anything. On Mother's Day 2007, an article spotlighted her and her baby daughter in the newspaper. She had dated the same man for over seven years when she gave him an ultimatum: "Give me a ring or it's over." This Red Flag Man obviously did not want to get married, but he did marry her when she forced the issue. Lacking the necessary commitment and responsibility, he later left her when she was six-months pregnant. Ending up with a broken home for her new daughter, she wishes she had noted the predictable patterns of her Red Flag Man sooner. Somewhere along the way, what she wanted so badly got in the way of who she was. Her clouded judgment dictated her unwise choices.

Love can happen, but be happy with yourself in the meantime. Couples seem to dominate the world, and yet many women in the United States are single. You have to find happiness within yourself, and then you can be satisfied with that before extending yourself to being part of a couple. What could be better than true love and devotion in action?

In my old neighborhood, there used to be an elderly couple that took a nice long walk every day at the same time. I had noticed them for months, with their silver hair, casual attire, and slow, comfortable pace. The unusual occurrence that caught my eye was that they tenderly held hands, constantly smiled, and seemed to be conversing happily with each other. Many older couples I noticed driving down the street or shopping in stores appeared to be grumpy, irritated, and fussy with each other, making me grateful for my single state.

One rare day I had a few extra minutes and spotted the happy couple. Pulling over to the curb at the side of the road, I got out of my car and cheerfully said, "Hello! Mind if I ask you a few questions?" They stopped and looked at me curiously and yet kindly. I explained that I lived in the neighborhood, had a big family, and walked along this same road myself. I continued to explain that I couldn't help but notice how lovingly and kindly they treated each other and how peaceful and happy they seemed. I told them they appeared to have the secret to a happy marriage.

They both smiled heavenly smiles. I can picture the Kodak moment as I write this. She looked lovingly at him, and he spoke first, explaining that he had been a minister, and religion had been an important part of their lives. They had been happily married for decades. She spoke of compromises, good attitudes, and consistently supporting each other. She mentioned their grown children and that she had stayed home to raise them and had enjoyed that.

Somehow their love did not die amid financial woes, problems with children, conflicts with in-laws, material-ism, television, sports fanaticism, and all the other things that seem to rip couples apart today. Their love only grew and matured to a beautiful stage that made them glow and beam with utter joy and delight. They really were enjoy-ing their golden years happily together.

What they displayed and lived was certainly nothing spectacular in the eyes of the world, but it was priceless. Their life had been about them as a couple, not about individuals and individual accomplishments. Asked if they would consider speaking to couples at our elementary school, they said they would. Life went on, I moved away, and never saw them again. All that remains is that impression of true and lasting love, and its very real possibility and promise on Earth despite tumultuous times. This couple exhibited a superior pattern worth emulating. They were both sure of themselves and of each other.

I asked a young woman why she thought so many women made such huge mistakes in choosing a man. She said, "They mistakenly go for what looks good or in other words, the outside package." I might add that they don't value who they are enough to look beyond that package. Hollywood has painted quite an impressive picture of being seen with a handsome man wearing a Rolex and driving a flashy car. Many experience undue pressure to date, marry, and have children. The movies, television shows, magazines, and tabloids paint an unrealistic, unattainable picture. Young women feel like failures if they don't meet the image portrayed everywhere in our society. If you are sure enough of yourself, you will be able to recognize such unrealistic propaganda.

Asking women why they ignore the obvious flags, they say they just did not trust their own instinctive warnings. They feel they are being too picky or are analyzing too much. They just don't trust themselves and seem to be lacking the necessary self-confidence to make good choices. They are sometimes desperate and so easily overlook and ignore critical characteristics. Please trust yourself. You know what is best for you. You know the truth of your situation. Now you just need the strength and courage to do something about it.

A woman recently told me that she had been rereading her journal. Months before her wedding, she was very unsure and worried about several issues. She saw problems in the relationship with her Red Flag Man, but she was not sure enough of herself to confront the issues. Unfortunately, she neglected to heed her own advice. If she had spoken to someone she trusted, perhaps the issues could have been faced and solved earlier and prevented her untimely divorce. Calling off engagements and weddings doesn't happen enough if you look at the divorce rates. She did not carry her journal-writing to the next critical step. Getting away and contemplating what you have written in your journal and highlighting areas of concern will help you recognize the problem areas and put a "hold" on the relationship. Doing so will be easier than the inevitable divorce down the road.

Introspection will help you define who you are and what you want. Open your eyes and see what is real, deep, meaningful, and important on the inside of a person. Open your ears and hear what is being said. Demand that it be respectful and abuse-free. Does anything in your relationship seem fishy or inappropriate? If you do your homework, watching out for any signs of a Red Flag Man, you will be able to taste and feel joy, happiness, peace, and life as it should be. Look beyond the clutter, smog, and mixed messages coming at you from every direction. Look inside yourself to know what is best for you. Listen to those who love you and desire to help you make the most of all that is you.

Know yourself before you settle down with a man.

Know yourself. Do whatever it takes to know who you are, and do it *before* you settle down with a man. You cannot be true to yourself until you know who you really are. Then, and only then, will you be ready to make the right choices in finding a good, worthy man. "First things first," my dear mother used to say. Know yourself and then be true. Analyze for a moment and think, *What do I do?* Then gather the strength and courage to go do it.

I remember hearing a touching story about how a man decided to marry a certain woman. He commented on being attracted not only to her outer beauty, but her inner beauty caught his attention, too. They both had leadership roles in organizations on campus where they attended college. They took time to get to know each other in the ways that really matter. Her stable and secure self-confidence made her even more desirable.

Over time, he witnessed her ministering to those in need in many volunteer situations. He had a good idea of her natural goodness from her service to others. That exemplified the kind of woman he wanted to spend the rest of his life with. She has been an incredible mother to their four children, and they have gone overseas to adopt more. Looking for the qualities that really count and matter shows character.

Goodness is more than skin deep. You need to go below the surface, past the designer clothes, body build, cars, jewels, and jobs. The things that seem to be impressive and worth a lot in the world end up not meaning that much. You should not be on the prowl for a man for financial security or just to avoid being alone. Furthermore, you need to put that biological-clock worry out of your head. Yes, you may greatly desire to have children and be a mother; but that is not sufficient reason to settle for a Red Flag Man. Be surer of yourself than that. There are things you can do to boost your self-confidence.

First know that everyone feels inadequate at least some of the time. Meryl Streep, one of the great film actresses today, commented on overcoming self-doubt by saying, "Fake it till you make it." Acting as if you have the necessary confidence will help you build it. Encouraging and energizing yourself with positive self-talk helps as well. Knowledge will help you see the importance of discovering your authentic self and then adapting your life to fit it with or without a man. If you do meet a man with inherent goodness, your lives can be joined for the right reasons, and you will never lose who you are.

Being with a Red Flag Man can be very risky and reason for pause and concern. Read those ten distinguishing characteristics again. You will see a pattern of selfishness and self-indulgence, not qualities you need to compliment being the best person that you can be. You will simply occupy space, provide services, and wonder why you feel so lonely and sad. If you see red flags, think long and hard. Nurture you own best self.

Take responsibility for yourself. The path towards greater self-confidence begins when you make you a top priority. Every step you take to improve your life will increase your belief in yourself. As you learn to rely on yourself, your self-trust is building. You may even consider a mentor or life coach. Confident people are happy to help.

Be sure of yourself by becoming an empowered woman and appreciating yourself. Know you can be happy single or married. Carefully consider all the consequences of your decisions. Make careful notes of predictable patterns and heed warnings. Save your tears for things that really matter. Love and trust yourself.

What do you do? Theodore Roosevelt offered some great advice when he said, "Do what you can, with what you have, where you are." Exercise control over what you can. Know how very special you are. But before you do anything, *be sure of yourself.*

Be Strong

*Like the elephant, we are unconscious
of our own strength. Wake up to your own
strength. Wake up to the role you play
in your own destiny. Wake up to the power
you have to choose what you think,
do and say.*

Keith Ellis

The weight-lifting kind of strength would be easy to accomplish compared to the inner strength of character needed to make good yet difficult choices that will determine your destiny. One young man exemplified such strength. While he was driving home from a late movie with four friends, one told him to stop the car. As he did, the three other rowdy high school hooligans jumped out of the car and proceeded to demolish a neighbor's holiday yard display, climb on her roof, and run around in her back yard. They had no idea her neighbor was watching and recording a license plate number. This young man was not very smart to withhold the evening's activities from his mother.

Monday morning, as the registered owner of the car, she got a call from a police detective. He told her about the vandalism report he received and that the driver of the car never left the car and did no damage. He was, however, guilty by association and had to pay the hundred dollars of his own money to cover the homeowner's damages. He reportedly was the only teenager of the group to look the victim in the eye, apologize, and sincerely care. The others deny the story to this day and have gone their separate ways. His mother remains proud of a strong son who learned a very important lesson that night and stayed in the car. You are going to need to be even stronger when dealing with a Red Flag Man. Forget the notion of the weaker sex.

Forget the notion of the weaker sex.

I have known so many incredibly strong women over the years. I recently had dinner with one who looked fabulous and had a very good job with a new, upcoming skincare company. Only a few years ago, she experienced enough tragedy to keep some women down and depressed for a lifetime. Not her. She showed exemplary strength to overcome all odds for herself and her three children. After she separated from her husband, he neglected to pay rent on their home for three months, and they were evicted. She had no money, no job, and no place to go. That did not stop her. However, she needed more than her inner strength to start over.

Here we-women-must-help-each-other-out comes into

play. A single woman let her move in, and friends helped her move. For a year, one child was in college, eating only one meal a day because the dad did not send him enough money, one child slept in the study, and another child slept on the sofa. She still has much to overcome and many financial battles ahead with their father. But she is determined, strong, and on her way to recovery. We women are certainly strong enough to have our own peaceful, wonderful lives. Remember, the human spirit is stronger than anything that can happen to it.

Another woman had an ex-husband who was lying in wait. Any experience you have with a Red Flag Man may return to haunt you even many years later when you least expect it, giving you even more reasons to exercise extreme caution with a Red Flag Man. This particular woman's first husband left her with two small children and was out of the picture for years and never sent a penny of child support.

A strong woman, she worked hard to raise her children on her own and had fun doing it. Her positive, great attitude helped her make the best of her situation. Years later, she met a wonderful, kind, and caring man. They married and started their new life. Her children saw their father in another city occasionally, but he was never a major factor in their lives. One summer this Red Flag Man, and absentee father, talked one of the older children into living with him. He took advantage of his son's vulnerability, every child's desperate need for his father. The mother experienced shock and devastation. The physical loss of the child that she had single-handedly raised was unbearable. But being a Red Flag Man, this father had not finished yet.

She got legal papers ordering her to pay him child support. Luckily, this friend was able to get her own good legal counsel and sued him for all the back child support he owed her. After a long, painful, nasty, costly court battle, she won in the end. She was very strong throughout the terrible ordeal. I believe that to be true for all of us. In the end, you will win if you are smart, strong, and do not give up.

You must always be on your guard, on high alert, even on level-red alert if a Red Flag Man is involved in any way. If you allow one of these Red Flag Men to invade even a tiny portion of your space, your life will never be the same. The effect can be hurtful and endless. You can get over it, but the lifelong scars are irreversible.

Compare this necessary alert to the ones at the airport. Just like the level red alerts at the airports, this level red alert can save your life and the lives of your unborn children. Don't have someone lying in wait to seize every opportunity to hurt you for the rest of your mortal life. Simply use what you know and feel to be strong, and make wise choices.

You cannot let your fears paralyze you. You may have inner fears of being alone, losing your children, raising them alone, or making it financially on your own. You have got to be strong, beginning by just putting one foot in front of the other and getting through one minute at a time. If you hold your head high, your confidence will soar. Watch out world, for here she comes! You will be down and out no longer. You will not be like a turtle hiding in its shell. You will bravely and self-assuredly come out and enjoy your life on your own terms.

An interesting situation happened early one morning while I was swimming laps. I had noticed a man coming early to swim. The lap lanes were full when he arrived, so he just went to the smaller pool right next to the lap pool. It is not ideal for laps. He gradually caught on that if he came earlier, he could get a good lap lane. Imagine his delight to finally get a lane after months of missing out. I thought, *this is going to be interesting.* He entered the lane no one dares enter. As the first person at the door every morning at 5:25 a.m., a certain woman puts up her clothes in her locker, gathers her swimming supplies, and gets in her self-claimed lane with the same ritual every day.

Words are not always necessary to extol messages. *What will she do?* As I swam up and down my lane waiting for her to show up, I continued to wonder. I should not have wondered. She boldly put her feet in the water and stood her ground strong and tall. Her stance alone said to the world, "This is my lane, and nobody but nobody challenges that, no matter what time they arrive!" She took off with her hands and feet splashing especially high. The unsuspecting man did not know what had hit the lane. She made no attempt to share, and they were headed for a collision.

He appeared a gentle sort of man, or perhaps he knew not to mess with a determined woman. He stood up to walk the rest of the lane, jumped out, and went back to the smaller pool. She pretended to stop and look around, as if wondering what had happened. I was surprised that he hadn't stood his ground and kept on swimming. She surely would have eventually moved over and shared the lane like everyone else. But he did not know that. Retreating is not an option for us as women.

Strength requires appropriateness. For days, I remained dismayed at her inconsiderate behavior. But her *intensity* to stand her ground can be a good example for all of us women. We need to be strong. Men do not need to wonder what a woman will do. They need to know with all certainty that we have the strength to stand up for ourselves and what is good and right for us. Being strong can be a great vehicle for good in this world. Let us be the strong, good women our destiny demands of us and live up to our true potential. Maya Angelou, author, poet, and women's advocate, said, "One isn't necessarily born with courage, but one is born with potential."

You are never too old to muster up the courage to be free of abuse. No age limit has been set. Consider this incredible story of a very courageous woman in her seventies. She had gone to the same hairdresser for a long time. The hairdresser noticed an unusual number of bruises and marks on her arms and face over the years. When questioned, the woman always made excuses that she had fallen or the dog tripped her. Eventually, she got especially close to her hairdresser and opened up to her one day. She faced age-old questions. "What now? How much more can I take?"

Her husband had been abusing her on every level since their marriage and subsequent raising of three children. She had no marketable skills and not a penny to her name. Finally, having been convinced that even in her later years she deserved to be treated lovingly and respectfully, she arranged for a place to stay with relatives in another state. She left with only the clothes on her back. Unfortunately, her three children who were grown and married did not support her. Be aware that this is not uncommon, making the lot of women that much harder in abusive situations. Courage shows firmness of spirit at any age.

Despite it all, somehow you go on. She expressed her deep gratitude to the friend that encouraged and supported her, and yet her personal courage and strength made the difference. Each of us needs to provide that same friendship and love to those whose lives cross our paths. This woman did it, and so can you. Author Alan Cohen explains, "There is no real security in what is no longer meaningful. There is more security in the adventurous and exciting, for in movement there is life, and in change there is power."

Another courageous woman exhibited great strength battling various cancers for over twelve years. She literally willed herself to live years past what the doctors predicted and endured treatments, surgeries, and extreme pain because of her great desire to finish raising her two children and be with her incredible husband who lovingly stayed by her side through it all. They meant the vows they spoke to each other, especially "in sickness and health."

Her only daughter moved up her wedding date when her mother's health started to decline drastically. They were able to do the mother/daughter planning and photographs, but even with the date moved up, it became evident the mother could not last until the wedding. The daughter wanted her mother to see her speak the same wedding vows her exemplary parents had spoken. She was in awe of their example and their tender, loving marriage.

They decided to have a pre-ceremony just for her mother. She dressed in her gown and stood with her dear fiancé while the preacher performed the ceremony at her mother's bedside. Many tears were shed, but obviously the wedding was what her mother had been waiting for since she passed away thirty minutes later. She is an example of a strong woman of courage who made a wise choice and left a legacy of love and commitment for her daughter and son. You, too, can muster the same courage to be strong and make good choices. Marriage is a luxury, not a necessity. You need to choose carefully and wisely.

A woman was controlled, manipulated, and watched over to the point of having no freedom in her relationship with her Red Flag Man. She was deprived of any association with her own family, affection, the ability to make her own decisions, and the basic freedoms we all take for granted. She loved her children, was a marvelous home-maker, and endured all the abuse for the sake of her family until gradually they all went off to college and started lives of their own.

Marriage is a luxury, not a necessity.

She found herself envious of them as they each left for college. The familiar was no longer meaningful and had not been so for years. Movement on her part had to be carefully calculated, and her courage grew along with her preparations. Finally as the last one left, she gathered all the courage in the world that she would need to leave. Her husband was extremely controlling and a powerful attorney, so extreme caution was required.

She audaciously prepared a plan and executed it daily when he was at work. She packed things that were special to her and stored them in the attic. She made arrangements for a place to live. When the time came, her leaving went well. She moved her few things and had the papers ready for divorce. He was furious. But she did it. She had problems with many of her children too, but we can only hope they will understand someday and that they will not repeat the deplorable example of their Red Flag Man father. Being strong may not be easy, but it is critical.

You will find that the courage you need will be there if you just take one important step, and that step leads to the next one. "Most of us have far more courage than we ever dreamed we possessed," said Dale Carnegie, motivational author and speaker.

The reward for strength and courage is *freedom* in many forms. Standing up for yourself sometimes becomes necessary in the workplace. I worked for a company that provided reading tutoring for private schools. The summer training was strenuous, but the great job paid well, and it could be done while my children were in school. I did not like the man who trained us. Looking back, he was a Red Fag Man being overbearing and intimidating. I quit after a year and could not get away from him fast enough.

Because I did a really good job, when an opening came available mid-year, the school principal requested me. When the tutoring director called me, I drew that line in the sand, having previously decided not to be treated that way ever again. I told him that his domineering treatment was offensive and unacceptable to me and that I expected to be trusted and treated professionally and respectfully. I refused to tolerate such demeaning behavior. There comes a time for you to realize this important fact and never back down. Even if it means a job, a spouse, a child, or whatever, you have to stand up for yourself. Knowing who you are, what you want, and what you will put up with takes a lot of courage. He turned it around; I took the job and had a great semester. You'll never know how others, even a Red Flag Man, will react until you set your limits and defend your rights.

I love springtime and teaching my students all the beautiful signs of this season. After studying the life cycle of butterflies, one student brought a huge, gorgeous moth to school. We got our books out and figured out how moths differ from butterflies. Because they were so interested in the live moth, this made for an extraordinary science lesson. We noted that its body was bigger, its antennae looked like tiny feathers, and it kept its wide wings open when resting. The sensitive boy who brought him expressed concern that he might die in captivity, so as a class we all went outside to set the moth free. Initially, the moth just stayed on the grass barely moving its wings.

Fearing it was near death, we put it back in the box, but the moth began fluttering again. Feeling confused, I decided to try letting it go up high instead of on the grass. What happened was amazing. The moth courageously spread its wings and flew in all its glory across the cloudy spring sky. The class broke into a huge applause. Seeing that moth fly in complete freedom and beauty brought home a message to me. With courage, what seems dead can come to life again.

That moth reminded me of us as women. Circumstances beyond our control, such as the moth's capture, often limit our existence. Our wings are injured, so to speak. We are low on the ground, barely moving. Though we feel only partially alive and probably appear partially dead, we still keep going. Moving around and doing menial tasks takes all our energy, as depression and despondency take over. There are many days we do not want to go on. Life just seems too hard and the tasks at hand too stressful and the efforts not appreciated.

We can gather some strength as the moth did, briefly on the grass, as it moved its wings halfheartedly back and forth. Our heart just isn't in it. We are too sad, too hurt, and too battered. We see no end to the pain and hopelessness. But we are like that moth, slowly but surely gathering courage, about to fly once more. As our resolution increases, our courage bolsters us, and life looks better. Within our souls, something whispers to us, telling us what we need to do now.

The seeds of courage are like a plant that blooms when the time is right. Times vary with individuals and circumstances. You may have the desire to be courageous before the strength to execute it has developed within you. It may take a series of unforeseen occurrences in your life to bring your courage to the surface and your life back to you. When the time and circumstances are right, you will be like that moth. Once in the air, you will feel the wind underneath your wings giving you strength and freedom in your soul, allowing you to soar. You will be filled with gratitude and relief for the glorious return to being yourself along with the joy of living and the courage of knowing that you can make it on your own. It is possible. It does happen.

You may wonder why you are still alive through times of

suffering or lack of purpose other than to raise your children under not very pleasant circumstances. Your mission is not complete as long as you are breathing. Granted you may barely feel alive for many years, and yet be alive nonetheless. The day will come when you will feel alive again and grateful for it. Like that graceful moth, you will be gliding along cherishing and savoring your freedom while working hard to deserve and preserve it. With that freedom, your new purpose and destiny begin. Whatever you endure shows your courage as you grow and mature through it. And then you can fly and meet your full potential. There is no age limit or timetable as long as you are alive.

Courage is a set purpose to go on in life. A man of ninety-nine years still reaches out and makes a difference in the world. Despite his age, he is able to deliver meals on wheels to shut-ins and regularly cheers them up. He could easily be home comfortable in his lounge chair watching television. Instead, he is courageously soaring by helping others and making a huge difference in many lives. Your mission is a work in progress, and it is going on right now. What you make of it is entirely up to you, and it depends on your daily choices, big and small. The strength you need is inside you waiting to evolve as it is exercised. Use it.

Aesop said, "It is easy to be brave from a safe distance." We naturally speak of bravery in wartime when soldiers are defending our country. As women, we also need to be bravely every day, just as we are in childbirth. We need to stand up for ourselves and for what is right, using all the strength we can muster. It is hard, but not impossible for women of all ages to be prepared for unexpected occurrences in our lives.

Recently, I was calling parents to remind them to send in necessary forms for our cumulative records at school. One mother said she refused to sign our Code of Conduct booklet. I was shocked and remained silent until she said, "Hello, are you there?" There have been many times in my life when I have been rendered speechless, especially when I have been unprepared or caught off guard and thrown off balance. This reaction works against you in many situations, especially with a Red Flag Man. He skillfully gets you into uncomfortable, tricky situations. The only way to avoid such results is to watch out for those red flags and be the strong person you can be.

Bravery implies enduring pain and hardship. Women exhibit remarkable bravery as they suffer through chemotherapy and fighting cancer. Though never having experienced cancer personally, I still try to help out and encourage these brave women. Speaking up, wishing them well, and letting them know that I care and love them beats just ignoring their plight. Another way to show courage in helping other women is to speak up when our friends need warnings about Red Flag Men.

One woman went to her thirty-year high school reunion. Discovering she was now single, many of her good friends said, "Thank heavens. None of us ever knew what you saw in him!" She wondered why none of them said anything. Perhaps they could have given her the strength to see the truth and spared her decades of torment in a Red Flag Man relationship. But would she have listened?

As women, we need to stick together and speak the truth as we see it. You may need to be brave when trying to warn a friend or loved one of possible red flags that you observe. Do not be afraid. Simply share your insights and concerns in a calm, nonconfrontational way. If they are unheeded, your support and love will be even more important later if her marriage falls apart.

I recently heard a lovely musical piece that reminded me of one of my favorite ballet recitals, and with seven daughters, I have been to many. It starts slowly. I can still see the older girls dressed in pale pink and wearing toe shoes as they come out from one corner of the stage diagonally crossing very slowly one step at a time. The vivid picture in my mind has often made me think of all the steps we take willingly and unwillingly, and yet ever so bravely in our lives. To quote astronaut Neil Armstrong as he stepped onto the surface of the Moon, "That's one small step for a man, one giant leap for mankind." Think about steps you have taken and where they have taken you. Some steps are more monumental and critical than others.

The happiest steps I can recall are when each of my children was learning to walk, watching those tender, brave baby steps as each one reached out to our open arms. We would all applaud and cheer for those monumental first steps. The cheers turned to tears as they took steps out the door to go to kindergarten and the rest of the school years. The giant step you take will be deciding whom you should marry. Slow steps down the aisle to get married should be the most joyous and happiest of times. If however, you make the wrong choice, those could be the last happy steps you take for a very long time.

Moving around freely can cease if a Red Flag Man takes over and doesn't allow you to be yourself. Even later, if you get free, you will pay a huge price to try to get your old step back. The saddest steps of all for many women suffering from divorce are of their children walking away and moving out to live with their father. Backtracking steps when they returned to live with their mother bring more struggles causing further fallout. Walking up and down the courthouse steps is difficult for women as they endure painful, expensive hearings and proceedings, often alone and very frightened.

Despair often sets in if you are not strong. Remember progress is bravely made one step at a time. One step forward, two steps backwards. Women stumble, trip, and fall down, but they somehow get back up and keep going. Initially steps become paralyzed. Friends, angels from heaven, help you through dark days. Stepping out into the workplace after many years at home can be mind-boggling and absolutely terrifying for women.

Somehow you will manage to take the first huge step and just keep putting one foot in front of the other. However, it could be even many more years before you regain the skip and exuberance back into your step. Slowly but surely, you can regain the desire to go on despite the confusion and trauma. Recovering from a Red Flag Man can be very difficult no matter how strong you are.

Women need continually to build up their inner strength to make wiser choices. Use lives of exemplary women to add to your strength. Muster the courage to stand up for yourself and be strong in all situations. Take life one step at a time, helping each other along the way. Drawing on your inner strength will give you the courage to be brave and recognize the dangers of a Red Flag Man, and then you can make wise choices.

Red symbolizes danger and "stop." If you see it and know what it feels like, then you need to be brave, courageous, and strong and do something about it. Perhaps having that knowledge will enable you to walk step by step on the pathway of a wonderful, fulfilling, and happy life free of abuse. You are stronger than you think. Sometimes that first step is the hardest of all. Consider your first step in the right direction. That is exactly what you need to do.

chapter seventeen

Be Safe

He who learns but does not think, is lost!
He who thinks and does not learn is in
great danger.

Confucius

Sometimes we suppose we are in a safe situation when we really aren't. One summer afternoon in high school, several friends and I went out for a sail on a beautiful lake. Unfortunately the wind subsided, leaving us on the other side of the lake with neither motor to get us back nor cell phone to call for help. We watched the gorgeous sunset melting into the clear, still water. Unknown to me, our little sailboat silently and slowly drifted towards the hazardous spillway.

Eventually darkness overtook us, and we appeared to be the only ones on the lake that evening. The guys might have been aware of our dangerous predicament, but I remained naively oblivious and enjoyed the reflection of the big, yellow moon flickering on the placid water along with our jovial, companionable conversation. Luckily, mere feet from the spillway, we heard a motorboat in the distance. My friend's father came to the rescue and slowly, methodically towed us across the lake back to the safety of the marina.

Being safe is an important issue. We are bombarded continually with safety issues in our daily lives, from car and traffic safety to food and product safety and everything in between. I remember when several of my children went to the circus years ago, and in one act, the performers missed the trapeze swing and fell to the safety nets below. It was traumatic to watch, and the performers suffered injuries, even with the nets to catch them. Safety needs to be in the forefront of our minds in all areas of our lives.

In a healthy relationship, you feel good about yourself.

In considering safe relationships, you especially need safety nets to protect you as well. The state of being safe means you are protected against any type of harm, including physical, social, spiritual, financial, political, emotional, occupational, physiological, or educational. The opposite of safety in these areas leaves you open to danger, error, and accidents.

Several toy companies have been in the news because of unsafe products produced in China and distributed in the United States. They used unsafe paint on the toys, but it wasn't detected until later. The fire inspector does his job properly and comes to our school periodically to check our fire alarm system and enforce the fire code for the safety of everyone at our school. Safety matters.

Playgrounds at school have changed over the years, primarily because of safety issues. The big, tall slides I enjoyed as a child have evolved into safer, lower, winding tunnels. At school, we still have a long list of playground rules for the safety of our students. The ways of staying safe naturally adapt to the times.

In the 1960s, dating was different and much safer than the dating scene today. I didn't have to worry about the date rape drug being slipped into my soda, but my parents did warn me of certain dangers and expected me to be smart and careful. The same goes for you today. Staying safe is important and warrants a concerted effort on your part. Warnings from those who love and care about you should be heeded.

I can think of a handful of young women I know at this moment who are involved with Red Flag Men and are thoughtlessly and obliviously drifting towards the danger-ous spillway. They are in unsafe, risky relationships. Grow-ing up near the lake, I had knowledge of the spillway and its dangers, but in the enthusiasm of youth, I did not apply or recognize the knowledge. As a woman today, you have more knowledge than ever, and yet you may still proceed recklessly in Red Flag Man relationships despite red flags flying everywhere. Your mothers are distraught having to watch you head toward disaster so determinedly. Why won't you listen and learn from your mother's experiences and mistakes? With Red Flag Men, so many risk factors accumulate to plague your safety while help is right in front of you.

Being safe entails more than just your physical safety. It includes feeling safe emotionally and mentally, and it extends to having a safe environment to exist and thrive in. Feeling safe allows you to be free to be yourself, explore your options, and live your personal dreams as well as enjoy shared adventures as a couple. Can you begin a life as a new emotionally couple sound with an interfering mother-in-law who lives a block away and frequently drops by unannounced? Is it morally safe to "shack up" and hope for a ring with no promises? Is it chronologically safe to give the best years of your life to a Red Flag Man who has made no commitment to you or your life together as a couple? Is it financially safe to pool your resources before marriage and share your credit cards and good credit? Many safety issues arise around the Red Flag Man.

How safe is a woman who is so desperate for a ring that she lets a Red Flag Man charge it on *her* credit card? One woman I know would say, "It is not safe or smart at all!" She recently had to sell the diamond ring that *she* paid for on EBay for a loss after the marriage failed. How safe is giving up and sacrificing all that you are and desire for a Red Flag Man who sacrifices nothing? Being safe in a relationship encompasses many issues and warrants your close attention.

The business world addresses safety issues with visual exams, chemical analysis, X-rays, trainings, instruction manuals, regulations, and evaluations. Women today need to be just as vigilant concerning safety issues in their relationships. You need to feel safe to open your heart and risk vulnerability in loving someone. Both participants need to maintain a safe environment for themselves and each other for love to flourish. In a safe, healthy relationship, you feel good about each other and yourself.

Being around my friends who have healthy relationships and have endured the ups and downs of life committed to each other is heartwarming. One such friend recently described her husband as wonderful but a workaholic. Over thirty years, they have compromised, worked out issues, and loved each other unconditionally. She sacrifices to watch football games with him, and he encourages her to go to museums and musicals with friends if he can't go. They are both safe in every way as they live together amicably and yet individually pursue different interests.

Unhealthy relationships have red flags that if heeded, can keep you safe. Physical or sexual violence can occur without provocation or warning in risky relationships. If you can answer yes to any one of these following questions, you may be at risk for domestic violence in your relationship and need to seek help with a therapist or a domestic violence advocate.

The questions you should ask yourself are straightforward and easy to answer. They are from a combination of the ways you are affected when you are with a Red Flag Man. Answering them honestly can determine your safety in a relationship. Does he tease you in hurtful ways? Does he call you names? Does he check up on you? Does he control your hair or clothes? Does he monitor your phone calls, mail, or checking account? Does he threaten to hurt your pets or children? Does he seem like Dr. Jekyll and Mr. Hyde? Consider your responses carefully as you are assessing your personal safety now and for your future.

The movie *Crazy Love* depicts a perfect example of seriously dangerous safety issues that can occur when you get in over your head with a Red Flag Man, sensing danger and yet choosing to continue the relationship. This documentary film relates the true story of Linda Riss and Burt Pugach, a New York City ambulance-chasing attorney. After seeing her sitting at a bus stop, he got her phone number and vigilantly pursued her. Following months of extravagant dating, she discovered he was already married and tried to break off the relationship. He never let go despite the fact that he was already married and she got engaged to another man. She found herself caught in a dangerous Red Flag Man trap. Mr. Pugach's determination that no one could have her if he couldn't led him to hire someone to throw acid in her face, leaving her physically marred and eventually blinded.

The question the movie poses is which one of them was the craziest. She ends up marrying him after he spends sixteen years in prison for his crime against her. This movie definitely adds food for thought to the line, "Love is blind." Watching the scenario unfold gives obvious reasons for the need to be careful around such Red Flag Men.

Physical safety for women today is a critical issue that continually needs to be addressed. The Red Flag Man is not just a danger to your mental and emotional sanity; he can be a very real danger to your life. What you need to do is be alert and aware of that fact. Domestic violence in our country has reached astronomical proportions, and that translates to safety concern issues for many women. Watch for signs of potential violence, and take them very seriously. Thankfully the numbers have decreased due to more shelters and much needed assistance, and yet this concern still remains a very real threat to your safety. Prevention remains a huge question mark. The key can be education and awareness as well as detection of characteristic behaviors along with professional assistance.

Some tragedies can be prevented. When focusing on a problem such as danger to your safety, nipping it in the bud before you even get into trouble always helps. Many accidents, illnesses, and other tragic things in life are totally out of your control and cannot be helped. You accept those things and just try to go on the best that you can, but with many Red Flag Man relationships, some problems can and should be helped and avoided for your safety. In many cases, blatant physical abuse doesn't start until after the marriage ceremony, but plenty of red flags were flying, warning of possible future dangers. If you suspect something is not quite right, it probably isn't, so you need to stop, think, and get help. Do your homework.

One good friend had no idea about the physical abuse that lay ahead for her when she married a diplomat and moved to his country. Not knowing the language left her totally dependent upon him, and he gradually took advantage of her vulnerability. He abused her verbally at first, and his temper fits increased in intensity and frequency. Before she knew what was happening, she had been pushed, punched, grabbed, and overtaken abusively, leaving her at a definite safety risk. With no family or friends nearby, she could only lean on her faith in herself and her personal strength and determination to survive.

She took positive action by taking courses to learn the language and was then better able to get involved in the community. Having a child complicated her situation gravely, but she finally mustered the strength to divorce him and provide a safe home for herself and her child.

While eating a taco salad recently, I noticed the sour cream tasted a little funny, but the salad tasted okay. I didn't have anything else to eat, and I felt hungry. More than once I thought that the sour cream did not taste quite right. Luckily I did not wake up in the middle of the night with food poisoning, but if I had, it would have been my own fault for not listening to my own warning system.

FDA warnings of contaminated foods alert us that we must be careful about what we eat and store food properly to avoid physical consequences. Similarly, we need to be cautious about taking unnecessary chances for our general and specific safety in relationships with questionable Red Flag Men. We can also listen to people who love and care about us who might sense such danger earlier than we do and before it is too late.

Choosing a marriage partner is an important life decision that tends to be taken too lightly these days. Why just keep on going when something tells you to stop? These Red Flag Men do not give up easily, and some like Burt Pugach never give up. You are setting an example for good or ill for your children. You should never allow a hand to be laid on you in an abusive way, nor should you ever be pushed or cornered. Red Flag Men often use intimidation to control and physically harm women, and this unacceptable behavior should not be tolerated.

Not tolerating abuse applies to words as well. You should not be talked down to nor put down in any way. The initial verbal abuse can and does easily escalate to graduated physical abuse: first cornered, then pushed, then slapped, on to becoming a punching bag. How safe would that make you feel? What should you do about it? Apologies and promises never to do it again are empty and meaningless words. And to think, all you have to do is be aware, realize the situation is abusive, and say, "No!" This is an obvious place to draw the line.

Your very life rests in your own hands and can be spared from abuse and even serious injuries or death if you are smart and watch for red flags. You will benefit by writing down your observations about your relationship in a journal. Often go back, reread what you have entered, and with a red marker underline anything that is of concern or not quite right to you. If you see red all over the pages and throughout the journal, remember that is your own personal, private, flashing danger signal. Your situation could easily escalate and get worse. Calling upon your own courage and strength will make it possible for you to evaluate and get out while you safely can.

Only then will you be free to go on with your own wonderful, abuse-free, lovely life. Relish the solitude. Enjoy the freedom. Be an incredible friend. Be a caring neighbor. Find a worthy cause and volunteer for it. Pursue your personal dreams. The only limits you have are self-imposed ones. Stand firm in your behalf. Be smart and be safe.

Do not be like the college coed at Texas A&M University in College Station, Texas, who tried to break up with her psycho boyfriend. He killed her when she went to his apartment, cut up her body, and barbequed her remains on his patio grill. Obviously, she had no idea how dangerous he was, or she never would have dated him in the first place or gone to his apartment to break up with him.

Alexandra Stoddard, one of my favorite authors, encourages us to take care of ourselves as well. I have read and savored every book that Alexandra Stoddard has written. She speaks eloquently to women and has had a powerful and positive effect on my life. I highly recommend every one of her well written, beautifully designed, inspiring books. In *Making Choices*, she addresses the options we women are faced with in our lives. The need to watch for red flags before making choices is paramount for many reasons, including our safety.

She encourages us to think everything through before making decisions. Watch out and beware. You need to be safe. She emphasizes that saying "no" is okay. She believes that we should not be afraid to say it more often. You may need to use that one, simple, strong word whenever you sense problems or danger where a Red Flag Man is concerned. That is one important way to remain safe. Start by just saying, "No."

Women of all ages have options available to avoid making huge mistakes. In speaking of marriage, Alexandra Stoddard warns that you need to become independent before becoming interdependent in a marriage. Being sure who you are before marriage remains smart advice. She adds that we have to remember that marriage is not a cure, nor is it a safety net to escape some uncomfortable home situation. You may only be getting yourself into deeper trouble. One bad mistake does not warrant another.

Waiting until you are older and more mature seems to be one answer to this problem. You need to be healthy emotionally yourself before attempting to join your life with a man. But if you do make a mistake, why remain in abusive, negative, dangerous situations? Certainly, immaturity and being too young top the list of obvious reasons for such poor, risky, and even unsafe choices.

Staying can often be the most dangerous choice. A personal trainer shared her story. In retrospect, she noted some of the reasons women stay. She mentioned the most obvious: shared children, and then financial security, transportation, health and car insurance, a place to live in a comfortable neighborhood, and school situations.

Are you really safe? Would a close friend agree?

In truth, she never should have married her Red Flag Man. Luckily she got out before her situation got dangerous. She cut her losses before the abuse escalated to a precarious level, but a multitude of challenges still await her. One of the greatest challenges will be raising her children. Her daughter recently asked, "Why did you have us with him? Why did you ever marry him?" Those are questions you never want to hear from your beloved children. Think carefully now so you won't have to answer later. She will continue to worry about the safety of her children when they spend time with their volatile Red Flag Man father. Your poor choices not only put you in unsafe situations, but they could also put your future children at risk as well.

Safety is a huge issue in our world today if video surveillance is any indication. I have become very aware of these cameras in the grocery and drug stores, hair salons, at major intersections, in the malls, and most definitely in banks and at ATM machines. If a video camera happened to record your life behind closed doors with a Red Flag Man, would watching it be cause for concern? Consider replaying in your mind things that have happened with your Red Flag Man, and then carefully analyze the scenes followed by reading between the lines. Are you really safe? Would a close friend agree?

The market is swamped with detectors of every kind. Radar detectors caution drivers if police are nearby. Smoke detectors are everywhere for the purpose of warning us of fire. Metal detectors are handy tools. When at the beach, I enjoy early morning walks. On big, popular beaches, scavengers appear with their trusty metal detectors. They slowly scan miles of sandy beach in hopes of finding marketable treasures for the local pawnshops. They seem very alert to their surroundings and carefully go to all the possible areas where beach goers might have dropped things. The detectors beep or flash when something is discovered. We women need Red Flag Men detectors to warn us of potentially dangerous men. If you allow it, your parents or close friends could serve as your detectors to warn you when you aren't able to see things clearly and accurately for yourself.

Attention to detail needs to occur in relationships. You are very alert when your favorite brand of clothing goes on sale. You check things out when you find an expensive antique treasure to make sure of its authenticity. For diamonds, you shop around, compare prices, and make sure to get a gemologist's report. You don't take chances on wasting your hard-earned money on fraudulent merchandise.

Material investments readily warrant our close scrutiny and cautiousness. Should you not expend the same or greater effort when deciding the fate of the rest of your life? Choosing a man to entrust your life, heart, and soul to should be a far greater process than it usually is. Your safety is just one of the many reasons.

Hindsight provides lessons for us all. Every woman I have ever spoken to who had their lives messed up by marrying a Red Flag Man says, "I saw the red flags way before we married, and I thought and hoped he would change. He never did, and it only got worse." How many scenarios do you need for proof of this fact?

I can recall only a very few cancelled engagements of people I have known. Women foolishly tend to just go ahead even if they know they shouldn't. Getting over a cancelled engagement is much easier than a life devastated by a Red Flag Man. You are alert to radar to avoid a speeding ticket when driving down a highway. You are definitely alert to messages on your cell phones or to flashing gates at railroad crossings. The weather forecaster is alert to all the changes in the weather all over the world. If you want to, you can be alert to red flags trying to warn and save you from unsafe relationships. You just need to look a little longer and harder. What is stopping you from being on alert to be safe in your own life?

Swimming one Saturday morning, I witnessed something interesting. Rules require having two lifeguards in the pool area. One is up on the chair, and the other relieves him every fifteen minutes. I noticed one limping. He needed help and support to climb up to the lifeguard chair. While swimming, I recall thinking, *I hope I don't need saving today!* He could not get down by himself, much less over to the pool to save anyone. The next swimmers who arrived had no knowledge of this problem. They saw a lifeguard at his post, and everything seemed fine. How safe was that?

Women are similarly misled with Red Flag Men. They seem so normal and fine most of the time. Others may see them in situations that you don't. We make excuses or ignore little things with the explanation that he is having a bad day. In reality, you have a brain waiting to be used and used more often. You also need to listen to those who care and try to warn you. Relationships are rarely what they seem with a Red Flag Man and can put you in an unsafe predicament.

My principal asked me to switch from teaching first grade to kindergarten, and I excitedly agreed. Having years of experience of what children need to know in first grade will make it easy for me to prepare them the year before. However, I have bought many books on kindergarten and researched the internet to help me prepare for a new assignment. Though I feel experienced and capable, I recognize the need for guidance through reading, training, and asking other kindergarten teachers at my school.

This book can serve as a personal guide and aid for you and help you recognize what could lead to trouble. Don't feel rushed when the rest of your life is at stake. Take the time you need to be sure. If you have any doubts, stop and back off to evaluate. You have what it takes. Then not only will you be happy, free, and peaceful, but you will also *be safe*.

"All fantasy should have a solid base in reality," said Max Beerbohm, English essayist. Laci Peterson lived in an apparently dangerous fantasy world and had no clue of the precarious situation she was in the middle of as she lovingly set up the nursery for her unborn baby, thinking they were a happy family. Scott, her Red Flag Man husband, lived a dual life with other women. He decided to get rid of Lacy with her unborn baby to continue his preferred lifestyle. He is in prison, one less Red Flag Man on the streets. However, others remain and can possibly be just as big a threat to your safety as Scott was to Laci's life.

First graders know the difference between fantasy and reality when I read stories to them. You should be able to know the difference as well. The perfect life doesn't exist, nor does the perfect woman or the perfect man. There is no riding off into the sunset on a white horse. Reality hits, and all "honeymoons" end. Then real life happens. The good news is that reality and real life can be great if we can shed all the unrealistic expectations that engulf us from the mass media and make wiser, safer choices. Sooner or later, you must face reality. Living in reality can give real meaning and purpose to life. Don't let relationship mistakes stop you from putting negativity behind you and going forth anew, happier and safer.

I recall a challenging situation that compares to how you might feel when unsafely caught up or entangled with a Red Flag Man. One of my older daughters was blow-drying the long, beautiful hair of a younger daughter. Somehow, she got several round curling brushes stuck in that hair all over her head just as we were all supposed to be leaving to go somewhere important. I rushed her up to the beauty salon nearby and begged for their help. After covering her head with peanut butter and several of the stylists working laboriously for an hour, they finally extracted all the brushes with a nice amount of her lovely locks. The process of detaching yourself from a Red Flag Man can be like trying to get entangled curling brushes out of a head of long hair. The process can also be demoralizing, frightening, and demeaning, but yet is often necessary for your very safety.

A flashing red sign catches my eye as I drive down a street close to my house. I'm intrigued as I read, "Open, Psychic Past Present Future." At times, each of us would love to open up her palms, look at the cards, see her life laid out neatly, and know for a surety what to expect. Wouldn't it be nice to have the past explained, the present reassured, and the future protected? I've read about phone-in psychics and readings sent monthly. It's probably a big business. People continually need help in their lives, but they regrettably look in all the wrong places. Women especially are vulnerable. No magic crystal ball or sorceress can make your choices, much less assure you of safe situations. However, this book can be like your own personal crystal ball to educate you so you can then discover your own answers and keep yourself safe.

Just as the red lights flash to catch our attention, red flags wave to warn us of unsafe situations with Red Flag Men. We also need to be aware of the good things to look for. Critical positive components to look for in a healthy, safe relationship are simple respect and unwavering honesty. In such a relationship, you are free to express how you feel and to talk things out without fear of reproach or condemnation. You feel good about each other and yourself. There is mutual appreciation and acceptance. If you are not free to be yourself, express your opinions, pursue your personal dreams, or maintain contact with your family and friends, then you are in an unsafe, unhealthy relationship.

Some red flags wave but still go unnoticed. Even if you don't have children of your own, you have seen children wearing those tennis shoes that have built-in batteries and a tube of light that flashes off and on around the base of the shoe when they move. The kids love them, and they really are cool.

The brilliant inventor of red flashing lights on shoes missed the red flashing flags surrounding a Red Flag Man. She was swept off her feet like many vulnerable women.

After being royally wined and dined, feeling loved and adored, she was whisked away into fantasyland just like a princess. After a few years, she realized she had made a terrible mistake with a proverbial gold digger of a Red Flag Man. She was bright, successful, and creative. She had made a fortune all on her own by inventing flashing lights in shoes, and yet she had missed the signs in this Red Flag Man.

Following their separation, he went after her and her money, breaking into her home and trashing it, demanding millions in a settlement, and harassing her. Restraining orders did nothing to stop his continual, threatening behavior. She will not feel safe for a very long time. She should have seen that Red Flag Man coming.

Another woman confided in me about how a caring friend really helped her. The women shared an amazing bond that extended to a rare friendship. This friend pulled her aside one day and asked if they could talk. She expressed her concern about the way her friend's husband treated her. This woman had been battling the issue alone and thought it was obvious only to her. In reality, an extra set of eyes and ears comes in handy. The more people who love and care about us, the better and safer we are.

Making and keeping friends has always been a top priority in my life. Somehow I have been blessed to be able to maintain all of my various friendships. In our high school, we had a safety slogan that read, "Friends don't let friends drive drunk." For the purposes of this book, let's change it to read, "Friends don't let friends miss red flags when it comes to men." Listening to loving, caring friends improves your life and even your safety. Warning your friends may be tricky and sensitive at times, but still possible when you see the dangers that they are missing. Friends watch out for each other.

Inaction is unacceptable. A true friend cannot and will not sit by and watch a friend destroy her life. A lovely friend of mine has been battling serious cancer for five years. I frequently sent her cheerful cards in the mail. She made a point of telling me how they brightened the day and cheered her spirit, finding something special in her mailbox. Never fail to do *something* to let your friends know you care and love them. You may make a huge difference someday.

When I moved, I had an angel-from-above neighbor next door. She has done all the things I did to help my friend and more. My friends have watched over me, helped me, kept me safe, and literally saved my life. Friends make all the difference. Life is indeed fortified by my many friendships. Be there for your friends. If you see red flags, try to warn them. If they try to warn you, listen to them carefully. That's what friends are for.

In considering your personal safety in relationships and life, thinking and planning ahead will always serve you well. Maturity and wisdom combine to help you make safer choices, but seeking reliable advice can often help you see the big picture. Be honest about who you are and levelheaded about what you are getting into with a Red Flag Man. Be alert and pay attention to details. Ask questions and listen to the answers.

As you realistically approach relationships, wisely use the knowledge you have accumulated to ensure your safety and personal happiness. Be alert to danger signs. Don't hesitate to help and allow help from family and friends who cherish you. Doing so will not only keep you safe but also aid you on the road to being prepared for your future.

Learning about the existence of Red Flag Men will help protect you as you figure out how to know him when you see him, how you are affected when you are with him, and what you need to do for yourself. You can get help, but ultimately the decisions are yours. If you see red flashing lights on the red waving flags, use your head and at least stop and think.

You owe it to yourself to at least consider your situation with a Red Flag Man. How many of these sad tales do you need to hear to stop in your tracks? Even the lady who invented red flashing lights missed the cue. Don't let the next woman be you. Slipping into fantasyland is dangerous for your health, well-being, and safety. Red flashing lights and flags should be noted and heeded.

Be Prepared for Your Future

It is never too late to become what you might have been.

George Eliot

A bright, self-assured, on-the-ball girl graduated from college in three years and took off for New York City to fulfill her dream of working there. She studied the Internet for months, searching for jobs and places to live. Unfortunately, she watched one of the Twin Towers go down out the window of the office where she worked. She married a man she met while there, and they moved to Pennsylvania for him to get a master's degree. She became a nanny for some Wharton professors while biding her time. Preceding their move to Texas, Neiman Marcus flew her to Dallas twice for interview sessions before offering her a fantastic job with a promising future.

They made the move in the summer, but her job didn't commence until November. She had time on her hands and creative thoughts in her head. Always having been imaginative and artistic, she began designing and making jewelry. On a whim, she took some to a specialty store where they accepted it, sold out, and requested more. The day before her stable job with health insurance and other great benefits was to begin, she declined the offer and decided to start her own jewelry business. Taking her future into her own hands, she set up shop in her spacious loft apartment.

Though she had valuable help and support from her husband, she took charge and full responsiblility of her new business. So much is spoken to us of planning ahead and planning for our own future. Such advice applies to you, single or married. You are admonished to be prepared with your finances, savings, health, insurances, education, job security, and retirement plans. That certainly covers a lot but not everything. There are essential qualities of character to be developed as well that will make all the other preparations for your future possible and easier. These traits define who you are and will allow you to do what you need to do for yourself.

My daughter's qualities of self-confidence and self-assurance allowed her to go ahead bravely into the future, eventually having her specialty jewelry in over two hundred stores all over the world. Women of all ages desperately need those same qualities, especially when faced with dealing with Red Flag Men and relationships. Such poise and confidence develop over time and with great effort on your part and prepare you for all aspects of your life, single or married.

Since returning to work full-time, I can't spend as much time in my yard, specifically my prized rose garden. Previously I had spent hours planting, arranging, and trimming. Recently, I walked to the mailbox, one particularly unusual day, and could not believe my eyes. In late November, my rows of rose bushes had a miraculous surprise for me in the form of a display of twenty huge, fragrant, multi-layered blooms. Hope, I thought. There is always hope. Miracles do happen right here in my yard in Dallas, Texas. Despite the disappointments, darkness, and gloom, hope and beauty find their way to us.

Despite darkness and gloom, hope and beauty find their way to us.

I cut the lovely blossoms and arranged them, mixing reds and pinks in various vases and placed them all over the house as a delightful reminder of the hope and beauty that miracles bring into our lives if we but notice and acknowledge them. Martin Luther King, Jr. said, "We must accept finite disappointment, but never lose infinite hope." Though we may have all endured disappointment upon disappointment, we must never lose infinite hope. As my rose bushes prove to me over and over again, hope and beauty prevail in life despite all of those terrible, unfortunate disappointments, some of which are unavoidable while others don't have to happen.

We must have high hopes for ourselves and our future. Constantly hearing of so many broken homes and destroyed lives in our country causes me concern and distress. I must turn my head and see the good men that are excellent fathers and husbands. And my hope for my children and for everyone is to seek and find the good wherever it may be. This is possible though not easy. We must not lose hope. But what do we hope for? What do you do? That is the question we all must personally seek diligently to answer. Our hopes for the future, at any age or stage in our lives, must be high, persistent, and determined despite ever-changing circumstances that are often out of our control.

In the living of life, especially after the devastation divorce brings, hopes change. You may have hoped for a fiftieth wedding anniversary or big family reunions at the beach. You may have envisioned yourself hand-in-hand as an elderly couple, welcoming your grandchildren into this world. For you to change or modify your hopes and dreams is difficult but does not negate the possibility of a great future. Change and adapt we must, in order to make the most of our future days. With those changes come much needed growth, maturity, and at long last, peace

And perhaps, even an end to pain. Emily Dickinson said, "Pain has an element of blank / It cannot recollect when it began, or if there were / A day when it was not."

You may have felt that way for entirely too long. For too many women, this pain has been their constant companion for longer than they can recall, not in a physical sense, but definitely in an emotional one. You can learn from the pain of others and be spared such suffering if you are willing to listen.

Consider the faith and hope of a little child. Many years ago one of my sweet daughters taught me a very important lesson about faith and hope, which I believe are not only closely intertwined but essential in preparing for our future. It is a lesson I hope I never forget and can keep vividly in my mind always. In one of the lower grades in elementary school, her teacher gave each child a baggie containing two seeds. They were to plant and take care of the seeds and see what happened. She took this assignment very seriously. Luckily we had "grow boxes" in the back yard with good soil and sun exposure.

She confidently took a little spoon, chose two spots, and planted her two precious tiny seeds. Then she got a little cup out and filled it with water from the refrigerator water dispenser. She took one cup of water out for one seed, then returned and did the same for the other. She did this faithfully day after day. With her tender loving care and persistent dedication, the little seeds sprouted and flourished.

Faith definitely precedes the miracle. I must admit I was surprised and had not expected the seeds to grow. None of my other children had been lucky with planting over the years. Her patience and diligence surpassed us all as those seeds took a long time to grow. Day after day she would water and check on them and report on their progress. She was one very self-assured, hard-working little girl. The future of those two little plants was safe in her capable hands.

One eventually became a sunflower that grew over ten feet tall. Finally the bloom appeared, and we were all ecstatic. The entire family had gotten involved by now. One glorious, sunny day the green blossom opened, revealing the magnificent sunflower turning its head upward towards the sun. We watched the flower over the course of the day as it followed the sun across the beautiful sky. But there's more.

Sometimes, we get more than we could have hoped for. Miracle of miracles, the other seed had grown into a large watermelon patch. We could not believe our eyes. Then one day a yellow blossom appeared, and we knew our melon was on the way. Two seeds, two miracles, and a life lesson had been implanted in all of our hearts. The melon appeared and grew. Then bugs took over, so we decided to harvest the melon. I have a picture of my daughter proudly carrying it into the house. We sliced it and tasted the red middle section. But this lesson was not about the taste. It was about the process, the life cycle of faith, hope, miracles, and one little girl's self-assured determination. Developing that trait in her youth helped her later in all aspects of her life, and it has served her well in making her future bright and positive.

The sunflower began to lean from the weight of the huge bloom. We decided to cut it and perhaps put it in water in the house. I tried a knife and then garden tools, but I was not able to cut it. I had to saw it off the stem because it was that strong and tough. It was hard to carry in and still leaned when we tried to display it. The bloom was bigger than my daughter's head and still heavy to hold, but we have a picture of all pictures from that day of days. The life lesson was there right before our eyes, but seeing a lesson and applying it in our future lives are two different processes.

Though life experiences may leave us in seemingly hopeless situations, hope remains in our very being, waiting until the day that it can sprout and grow inside us once more. Your inner hope, though dormant for the moment, has potential and can come forth to help you along the way and bring you the peace that you so deserve

My daughter was the only one in her class of over twenty-four students that had growing results. She beat the odds. She not only had results, she had astounding results. Each day is full of new chances. Just keep the faith and hope will abide. You can have outstanding results in your life too, now and in the future, if you use the knowledge you've gained, make wise choices, and prepare adequately. Knowing that and believing in it is something you can do and be patient with yourself while doing it.

Patience is a virtue. As we patiently persevere, we will

find the strength we need to overcome difficulties and obstacles in our lives, even a Red Flag Man. Patience pays off. There are so many things that we have to wait for. Some things just cannot be rushed. You are stronger than you think, and you will be okay. Patience is just another of those essential character traits you need to develop now to ensure a better future later.

One woman tried to remain upbeat and positive despite the bleak circumstances she found herself in following her Red Flag Man fiasco. She struggled to raise her children alone, battled financial setbacks, and worked hard to make it all happen. She could not see any hope for her future because she was so bogged down with the everyday trivialities. She barely made it through each day, leaving no time for preparations for her future. Yet, she was strong, and she survived. She was the recipient of unexpected good fortune which lightened her load, returned her hope, and ultimately allowed her to get a peek at a better future. She would agree that her new and better life was worth waiting for, and the lessons she learned along the way were invaluable in building her character and expanding her compassion for others.

Quick fixes spring leaks. Ours is a new generation of quick fixes. An ad on television shows a man plugging a hole in a dam with some bubble gum. Consequently, the wall comes down later because quick fixes just aren't the answer. My students don't normally display patience. They want things *now*. Video games respond immediately.

There is no quick or uncomplicated fix after a Red Flag Man enters your life at any level.

Dallas has an art restoration store that can make broken Ming vases look like new. The repairs are expensive and take a lot of time. Recovering from a Red Flag Man can happen, but you will never again be anything like new or the same person you were. The passing of time will eventually ease the intense pain and allow you to proceed cautiously into the future that you must prepare for. When you add wisdom to that patience, you will realize everything you need is within you and your future can be bright.

Be ready to dance again.

Be ready to dance again. My intense love of music led me to volunteer to be Diana Ross for our school Black History Program. At the first practice, I overheard some snickers from some older kids, and I panicked. What on earth had I volunteered for and why? I was to sing and dance on stage for six hundred students, teachers, and visitors. I lost my nerve and tried to back out. The director would not allow it and said, "I'll get you a wig."

Life will go on with or without you. Sometimes we must be our own cheerleaders. Thursday came, the day before the program, and I was distraught. I procrastinated going over the song and practicing some dance moves, and I went to bed early. I awakened at 3:30 a.m. and went into survival mode. I got my outfit together and played the song over and over again until I felt comfortable with it. The time arrived, the moment of truth, the song started, and out I went onto the stage.

The students backstage were very encouraging and supportive. I really had fun. I rejoice that I faced my fears and went on with the show. Dancing is good for the soul.

One teacher said, "You think you know someone!" Another said, "What a show. You go girl!" I later told one of my daughters that it was just another big step onto the stage of my new life, a having-more-fun step. A dance-as-if-no-one-is-watching attitude. The I-have-confidence-in-myself mode can encompass you as you grow stronger every day. You can get stronger as your self-assurance builds and grows, making your future look much brighter.

You cannot dance until you are free to be yourself. Your fears are certainly much more serious than having to sing and dance onstage at a school program, but the same process of gathering courage and taking action needs to happen. There is nothing wrong with you if you find your-self under the spell of a tyrannical, abusive, domineering, controlling, and seemingly "wonderful" Red Flag Man. You are not the reason if he exhibits violent tendencies and treats you inappropriately. You deserve better than that now and in the future.

You know the truth despite what others may think, judging from outward appearances only. Granted, your wrong choice got you there, but now your wise brain can do something positive about it. If your present is not good now, what does that say about your future with a Red Flag Man? There is no need to suffer needlessly. Stop, work on it, get help, but don't just let it go.

No partner is needed to join in dancing for the pure joy of living. While teaching, I met the loveliest lady at our school who was labeled "an old maid school teacher." At seventy-five, she still proudly used "Miss" as her title. She taught many years, retired, and then substituted often. She always had her beautiful hair perfectly coiffed, her make-up was impeccable, and her posture was that of a balle-rina. There were no stress lines around her eyes, mouth, or forehead. Her skin was like porcelain. She dressed in colorful, stylish outfits and always wore the biggest smile. She waltzed cheerfully down the halls of the school say-ing, "Good morning to you. Isn't this the loveliest day?" She would smile with eye-to-eye contact from left to right at every person she passed. I remember thinking, *What is up with her?* Then, pondering her sincere, consistent hap-piness, I wondered, *What is her secret to life?*

What is in your heart shows in the expressions on your face. She could have been miserable or unhappy for a hundred reasons since she never married or had children. Instead, she devoted her life to helping many children. She chose to enjoy her life, have a great attitude, and make a difference in generations of lives. She spread cheer wher-ever she went. She was blissful just to be alive. She would sing and do little dances for the younger students when she taught them. What can you do? You too can dance on your own. Dance for joy. There is something to be said about the power of a positive attitude and that self-assurance it exudes. What better way to head into your future?

Have your dancing shoes ready. Being prepared, you will be able to get back on the right foot. You are then on your way to dancing again very soon. You will know when the glorious time to dance again arrives. There is light after dark, day after night. The possibility and option of coming back to life and being your old self again lives within you. You can arise and head into the future with a firm resolve never to take any type of abuse again as long as you live. The unspoken desire of your heart, to live again and to be free of it all, will finally surface and take flight. A glorious combination of patience, hope, and hard work will allow a rebirth to happen for you and will help you prepare for your magnificent future.

Consider the lessons growing roses presents. I have learned many important life lessons from my various rose gardens over the years. The first was that I could grow them although I was not an experienced gardener. My first attempt met with success. I learned to feed and prune them, and I enjoyed beautiful blooms that I placed all over the house and shared with friends and neighbors.

I quickly learned that putting in just a little effort brought forth amazing results and that it wasn't as hard as some people had wanted to make it seem by discouraging me. I am still amazed at how dead and ugly the bushes appear all winter long. A new miracle unfolds every spring, as the tender bushes leisurely come to life. I rejoice as each tiny leaf and bud appears. Then I have to stop and catch my breath when the first bloom meets my eye. What a glorious feat. The spring blooming is the freshest, most vivid, and abundant. The rows of bushes are covered with heavenly blossoms and look like a Monet painting draped along the fence.

Bloom where you are planted. That is another lesson from my rose garden. If we just take the time to notice, life is full of unexpected surprises. What do you do? I expand my garden and add bushes every spring. One year I almost tossed out a terrible looking bush, but at the last minute I decided to move it and stick it in a corner where it would get more water from the sprinkler system. I had the biggest surprise when it flourished on its own over several years and was covered in lovely pink blooms. Another lesson from the ashes is that hope springs eternal, even when it seems impossible.

My home-grown roses last much longer than store bought flowers. They last at least a week in vases all over the house. Their stems are strong. I check on the bushes every day, looking for any signs of disease. I have treatments on hand, and I mark my calendar as to when to feed them every six weeks. Yet, another lesson is that anything worthwhile is worth working at. Hard work pays off now and in the future.

A rose is symbolic for me. May we all have the strength of the bush that I didn't think would live. And may you have unexpected surprises in your life to add joy and true happiness. As you work very hard to make good choices, you will make a great life for yourself. I am a proponent of marriage when it is with the right, respectable, innately good, and honorable man. If that is not possible, you can live a full and wonderful life on your own. You can even be a "Miss" like that wonderful teacher and bestow happiness on the world. As human beings, we are not like the baby spiders in *Charlotte's Web* that float randomly and go wherever the wind blows them that particular day. You determine your future, and you have everything you need within you to do it and do it well. That is what you can do. Be prepared for your future.

One day I placed a sweet-smelling rose in a vase by the door in my classroom. I couldn't help but notice the students joyfully sniffing as they passed by. They inhaled that delicious fragrance, closed their eyes, and smiled delightfully. Watching them made me think that we all want what is sweet, beautiful, and exquisite in life. That moment can extend for a lifetime. We can be like that rose, patient, strong, hearty, and magnificent. Our choices will determine it. Take time to stop and smell those fabulous roses. The life you desire and the life you deserve can be yours.

"Be miserable. Or motivate yourself. Whatever has to be done, it's always your choice," said Wayne Dyer, inspirational writer and speaker. Changes occur as life takes twists and turns. The life I am living now is not what it started out to be, nor was it my plan. I think most people could say that to some extent. I envisioned something totally foreign to what I am experiencing now. You have to put the past behind you and look joyfully to your future. Married or not, many things change as the years go by, and you adjust and adapt.

When Plan A is no longer an option, as traumatic, tragic, and sad as it is, we have to go on to Plan B. Sometimes many things must be finished and years must pass before we can totally go on to the new plan. That could mean finishing raising children, going back to school, reentering the workplace, relocating, and totally reestablishing ourselves as single. The task, though enormous, can be accomplished despite your intense pain and emotional upheaval. This terrifying, though purifying, metamorphic process comes with a promise of hope for a new and better future life when the time is right and you are prepared.

You may be caught in limbo indefinitely and feel as if you belong nowhere. There will be a time when you can box up that life that was Plan A and put it on the shelf just like they do in *Cold Case*, the television series. They mark on the box in big red letters, "Case Closed." You could risk having to do the same thing if you get mixed up with a Red Flag Man. Some of the cases on the show take twenty years to solve. It could easily take that long for you to close your "case." The same applies to you if you make wrong choices. It could be years before you get your life back again. But when the time is right, you will know and will rejoice. You can make it. Rest assured that Plan B will be great for your future and maybe even better than Plan A ever was or could have been.

You can find a bright spot if you search. *Pollyanna* is one of my all-time favorite classic movies. What a perfect example of inner self-assurance in full bloom despite difficult circumstances. Books have been written attesting to the power of a positive attitude. I love the "glad game" she plays. It is a game you need to play especially when switching to Plan B. I like to call my game, "What's good about it?" One particularly busy week, I had my usual rigorous routine plus extra meetings every evening. As I walked out of my last meeting very late, I looked up at the beautiful evening sky and saw the most glorious crescent moon. It looked just like the one in the nursery rhyme, "Hey Diddle Diddle." I said, "That moon is what is good about this night!"

Under normal circumstances, I would have been inside at home, and I would have missed seeing that incredible, haunting moon. As you think positively, possibilities open for you. We might as well be upbeat about our situation. We cannot be looking down at our feet, nor can we keep our head buried in a pillow. We must put our shoulders back, look straight ahead, and be ready for our future. The good thing about today is that you are alive and able to pursue some plan

But you have to pay attention. Some things actually

pass us by because we are not focused, causing us to miss out. One cold, dark morning while driving to school early, I took an alternate route because the major freeway had a backup. I often look around as I drive, think about things, and sometimes talk on the phone. Thank heavens it was too early for that this particular morning. And gratefully I was looking straight ahead and going a little slower than usual as I went through a green light.

As I drove up to the light, which was also a bicycle trail crossing, a man on a bike rode directly in front of me. I smashed my foot on the brakes and held on to the steering wheel for dear life. My car literally came to a stop mere inches away from the man who had subsequently skidded sideways onto the road and fallen down on his bike. Before I could speak, a policeman appeared right behind me, got out of his car, and checked on the man. My past and future life flashed before me. As it turned out, the biker was fine and explained that his brakes had failed so I had done nothing wrong. He got up, dusted himself off, and rode on across the street as if nothing had happened.

I drove on to work, but I was shaking from the near accident. I cringe to think what might have happened if I had been on my cell phone. I could have run over that man and killed or seriously injured him. You have to *pay attention* to what is going on in your life. You have to watch out for danger in the form of red flags to avert disaster.

What do you do if you make mistakes? You bravely can

and must be ready, when the timing is right, to go on with another plan even if you are alone. To be alone is okay. Plan B is okay. "When one door closes, another opens, but we often look so long and so regretfully upon the closed door that we do not see the one which has opened for us," said Alexander Graham Bell, scientist and inventor.

Closing the door to Plan A will not be a pretty sight. It is a door, perhaps, that never should have been opened to a Red Flag Man. Many women experience terrible, ongoing nightmares of their husbands leaving them and their children. Some pains can never be forgotten. Red Flag Men move on very easily, and they go emotionally first, so that the physical exit is almost anti-climatic. The overwhelming symbolism of that final door being shut in front of you changes everything in an instant. You are faced with Plan B, like it or not. Turn and confidently face that new door to your future that is opening just for you.

Yes, you are left on the painful side of the closed door, but your choice put you there. After that first door shuts, regrettably there are many to follow before that new one opens. Even the bedroom doors of your children will slam shut in anger. When you have to sell the house, they will hold their doors shut and scream, "Go away. This is my house." The country club door is locked to you. Then there is the changing association with all your "couple" friends as those doors gradually close. The door to the bank is definitely closed, as is the door to the SUV. All those closed doors are a small price to pay for freedom from a Red Flag Man. Hopefully you don't have to learn the hard way that some doors are better off never opened in the first place.

Release it all when you can, and then open your eyes to a new chance and a hopeful future. Put your hand on that doorknob and close it now firmly and assuredly. Lock it and throw away the key. Then turn and open a new door to a possibly better life. There is hope in sight. Take heart. You can do it. Plan B awaits you. All those things that you always wanted to do but couldn't because of him await you. Success can be yours, as you hopefully, patiently, and attentively consider all your options, and then make wise choices. Happiness can be yours. With hope and courage, open your eyes to the miracles all around you. Your new self-assurance will serve you well in knowing what to do. A future dance awaits you.

Being smart, self-confident, strong, and safe all lay the foundation for living. To be prepared for your glorious future means having faith and hope. You will also need patience as you accept changes that inevitably occur and a willingness to consider Plan B for your happiness. Conquer your fears, always be ready to dance, and expect miracles.

Wisely use the knowledge you have gained to consider your options, draw the line at the appropriate time, and then stand up for the abuse-free quality of life you deserve. You enter this world alone, and you leave it alone. An amazing woman I met while waiting for a delayed flight at the airport said to me, "You came into this world an original. Don't leave it a copy."

Embrace life without fear. Take comfort in the fact that with this newfound knowledge, you will know the Red Flag Man when you meet him and you will know how you are affected when you are with him. Once you discover this Red Flag Man for yourself, you will be able to walk boldly into your future on your own two feet, knowing you are prepared to make wise choices.

If Only Daughters Would Listen to Their Mothers

It is the province of knowledge to speak,
and it is the privilege of wisdom to listen.

Oliver Wendell Holmes

"If only I had paid better attention." Those words spoken by a teenage girl will never leave her mind or heart. She promised to watch her little brother while her mother went to the store, but she got involved in talking to her friends. When she noticed him gone, it was too late. He drowned at the bottom of the swimming pool.

My youngest daughter, the one that provided me with the "happy baseline" her senior year of high school, recently left for another year of college. As we were talking before she left, I explained the precepts of my book. She turned sweetly to me and sincerely said, "Mama, what do you want me to know?" Mentally trying to condense my book, I searched for the most important, critical points to explain while I had her undivided attention. Looking back, I realize I never mentioned the Red Flag Man, but I focused on her and what she needed to do to protect herself. These were the brief points I stressed to my daughter. They are insights every mother wants her daughter to know and accept.

"Know how very special you are and that you deserve to be treated with the utmost respect. Don't be blinded by emotional love. Be smart. Use your brain. Stand firm in your moral beliefs. Be strong. Be aware of your surroundings. Be safe. Don't waste your young life wishing you were with a man. You have the world at your fingertips, so make the most of all the opportunities available to you. If you meet the right wonderful person, great, but if not, that is great too. Make the most of your life, single or married. Don't let the glitz and glamour of a wedding blind you to the reality of married life. Make sure you choose wisely."

She listened intently and nodded with understanding; we hugged tightly. Then it was time to continue packing. If only every girl would turn to her mother and ask, "What do you want me to know?"

You have gained significant knowledge which can heighten your awareness and help you define lines. You know more about the respect you deserve and need to defend. Now I must ask, "Will you *use* your newfound knowledge to make better, wiser choices in men?" You are a vulnerable, open target when the Red Flag Man turns on his beguiling charm, assaulting you from every possible angle and side. Mark Sandel, director of the Family Place in Dallas, Texas, explained that the common thread of all Red Flag Men is that when they put on their absolutely "charming" veneer that disguises multiple red flag warn-ings, he can easily see "how their wives would fall in love with them." Easily, yes. Wisely, no.

All your knowledge added to your strength and char-acter still may not be enough to protect you from an unfortunate onslaught from a Red Flag Man. You must be smart if you want any chance for personal happiness by using your heart, brain, and your *mother*, with all the valuable experience she brings. She may just be the one objectively, carefully, and gently to tweak your perspec-tive while making you aware of factors you cannot see clearly. She can help you ultimately discover the truth for yourself. Getting help in "seeing" those reasons and aiding you in your personal discovery is smart.

"The only real mistake is the one from which we learn nothing," said author John Powell. You have much to learn from the mistakes of your mother *if* you will but listen. You can benefit from ageless lessons learned. Courageously use the experiences of others, especially hers. So much rests upon your wise choice of listening, assimilating, and then discovering for yourself. Having support feels good.

My next door neighbor and I agreed to watch out for each other and our homes as crime has become a concern in our area. We decided to call each other day or night if we were afraid or concerned. I called her early one morn-ing when I heard her husband's car alarm going off. She said things were fine, so we laughed and went on with our day knowing we were not alone. You are not alone when working out your relationship issues with a Red Flag Man.

I recently had the privilege of having my third daughter here for three weeks with her precious one-year-old. Noticing her protective, nurturing guidance of her little one has made me proud. This little girl has a mind of her own already. Her senses are so alert, and nothing escapes her eager, bright mind. As she needs her mother now to keep her from walking into the street or eating off the floor, she will need her just as much later, though for entirely different direction and guidance. Girls need their mothers.

Don't let the alluring sound of potential wedding bells drown out the sound of your mother's voice of warning. *I Me Wed*, a Lifetime movie, takes on an interesting concept in a story about an attractive thirty-year-old woman who has grown tired of everyone asking her if she ever plans to get married. The resultant pressures cause her to plan an entire event of marrying herself. Your desire to have a wedding day and all it entails should not be the result of peer or family pressure or just personally settling and marrying the wrong Red Flag Man for erroneous reasons.

There are so many other ways to celebrate you, your talents, and your future life than staging a wedding that shouldn't be and then ending up in the sterile, crowded divorce courtroom. Strive to be happy and productive on your own, and then, if the right man comes along, you will be that much healthier and better off. Meanwhile, you have knowledge about the Red Flag Man and how you feel when you are with him. You have a loving mother, family member, or friend longing to help you see what you might have missed. What you do with what you have is totally up to you.

Denying your innate rights as a human being and compromising yourself in any way with a Red Flag Man would be a disservice to yourself. Seriously consider *what you deserve* and whether it is happening or possible with a Red Flag Man. You deserve to come home to a place of peace and comfort, not one of teasing, tormenting, belittling, and control. Your mind deserves to be free and open, not made to feel crazy and confused. Your eyes deserve to see smiles and approval, not angry frowns and disapproving glares. Your ears deserve to hear loving, kind, encouraging words and pleasant greetings, not tirades of put-downs, constant criticism, or grueling questions. Your arms deserve loving embraces and to be raised in the delight of living, not to be grabbed, pulled, twisted, yanked, or raised to block a hit. Your hands deserve to be held gently and lovingly, not pulled, tugged, grabbed, or raised to block your ears from verbal assaults. Your legs deserve to take you where you need to go, not to be kicked under the table to hush you. Your feet deserve to walk peacefully along the path of life, not tiptoe or walk on eggshells in constant fear.

The decision is yours to make with the help, love, and knowledge that your mother offers to you. Additionally, *Beware the Red Flag Man* can help by preparing you for better choices. Personally assessing how you feel emotionally, mentally, and physically when you are with a Red Flag Man may be harder to do on your own. Acknowledging how you are affected when you are with him can be difficult, but it is a necessary step before you decide what you need to do.

A woman knelt at her mother's gravesite as she lovingly placed a bouquet of her favorite flowers on the headstone. In contemplative thought, she wondered about her family's divorces: her mother, her own, her two brothers, and finally several of her own children. Nine families were broken apart and the lives of twenty children adversely affected. She thought, *They were all Red Flag Men. When and where does it end?* With tears rolling silently and slowly down her face, she quietly said, "Oh, Mother, you were right. *If only* I had listened to you."

Knowing her mother forgave her and lovingly understood comforted her. Yet having seen and experienced her own dreadful pain and that of all the innocent children involved for decades, she wondered if she could ever forgive herself. Shaking her head, she knew she never could. Just as she knew the pain would never really die until she did. My experience has shown me peace can be found even though the pain remains.

Don't let that woman be you someday. Instead, take heart and courage that you will recognize a Red Flag Man if he comes your way or is already in your life. And when you do, you will make the right choice and turn with dignity and self-confidence toward the bright and shining future that you desire and you deserve.

He [she] who chooses the beginning of a road chooses the place it leads to. It is the means that determines the end.
Harry Emerson Fosdick

Red Flag Man Checklist

It's important that people should know what you stand for. It's equally important that they know what you won't stand for.

Mary Waldrip

*J*ust as a runny nose, head cold, body aches, and fever signal illness such as the flu, certain symptoms readily and predictably forecast problems and trouble in relationships, especially when a Red Flag Man is involved. Carefully and, most importantly, honestly look over these questions and see how many of these symptoms apply to you and your relationship.

Check each question if your answer is "yes" and then calculate your Red Flag Man score.

- ❏ Are you the only "honest" one in the relationship?

- ❏ Has being with him compromised your personal honesty or integrity in any way?

- ❏ Have you experienced even the slightest lack of trust in him?

- ❏ Have you noticed a lack of open respect, support, and nurturing of each other in his family?

- ❏ Is unjustifiable sacrifice demanded of you concerning him or his family?

- ❏ Do you notice any unhealthy, abnormal, or inappropriate family attachments?

- ❏ Is he often overly preoccupied or too focused on himself or material possessions?

- ❏ Does he have expensive habits, hobbies, or collections that dominate his life?

- ❏ Do you feel controlled or dominated to the point of losing any of your basic freedoms?

- ❏ Are you just pretending things are great, hoping they will be some day?

- ❏ Does the way he speaks to you make you feel dominated, dependent, or inferior?

- ❏ Has he caused you to be isolated from your family or friends?

- ❏ Are you ever the brunt of unacceptable, often cruel, degrading jokes or demeaning comments from him?

- ❏ Has he openly threatened you or ever caused you to fear being physically harmed?

- ❏ Do comments he makes often throw you off balance and catch you off-guard?

- ❏ Has he ever said to you, "I know what you are thinking or feeling"?

- ❏ Does he have a negative, passive-aggressive demeanor or seem difficult to get along with at times?

- ❏ Are extreme demands made of you while he appears to do nothing?

- ❏ Do you even suspect he is already married?

- ❏ Does your affair require you to date in secret?

- ❏ Do you feel you have lost your personal identity because of being with him?

- ❏ Do you feel emotionally anxious, frazzled, or insecure around him?

- ❏ Do you live in fear of displeasing him or of his wrath?

- ❏ Does he habitually keep you waiting because he is always late?

- ❏ Does trying to discuss important issues get you nowhere?

- ❏ Do you find yourself hiding how you really feel from yourself and others?

- ❏ Has being with him made you seriously question your sanity?

- ❏ Has his personal power taken over your personal mental state?

- ❏ Could your battling TMJ, anxiety attacks, sleep problems, or depression result from being with him?

- ❏ If you watched a video of your relationship taped behind closed doors, would it reveal cause for concern?

- ❏ Does he seem like Dr. Jekyll and Mr. Hyde?

- ❏ Does your gut feeling tell you something just isn't right?

YES TO FIVE

You may certainly be with a Red Flag Man and need seriously to consider your answers and even discuss your concerns with a parent or trusted friend.

YES TO TEN

You are most definitely with a Red Flag Man and may even have serious problems already. You need to seek help from a counselor or therapist in addition to friends and family.

YES TO MORE THAN TEN

Your situation calls for immediate action on your part because you may be in danger in more ways than one.

Beware the Red Flag Man has been written to help you understand the complicated characteristics of a Red Flag Man; how to recognize his impact on you emotionally, mentally, and physically; and what you need to do for yourself. Be smart. Be sure of yourself. Be strong. Be safe. Be prepared for your future. Listen to your mother.